HOW NOT TO BE A C***T

AN INCONVENIENT GUIDE TO BECOMING A DECENT HUMAN BEING

J.C. ABI-SAAB

Hembury
BOOKS

ABOUT THE AUTHOR

John Abi-Saab has spent more than thirty years studying power inside classrooms, courtrooms and ministerial offices – rooms where reputations are made and decisions are buried. For decades, he has watched institutions talk about values while quietly doing the opposite: as a teacher in some of Sydney's harder classrooms; a lawyer defending the indefensible; a political adviser to ministers who regularly needed saving from themselves; and an administrator managing the ego collisions of international sport.

An Australian with Lebanese ancestry, John also understands the corrosive effects of power on the global scale. Once known as the Paris of the Middle East, Lebanon has been gradually consumed by corruption, cruelty, cowardice and entitlement. Its history informs John's belief that societies do not collapse in a day. They erode when enough ordinary people decide that the social contract no longer suits their narrative and the rules are for someone else.

It is this perspective which shapes his satirical debut book, *How Not to Be a C**t*.

John's surname, Abi-Saab, translates from Arabic as "the Father of Difficulty". It has proved less a name than a working description.

Living in Sydney with his wife, John spends much of his time drinking coffee, hiking in the natural environment, and following rugby union with the conviction that it is the only true form of rugby.

A catalogue record for this book is available from the National Library of Australia

CONTENTS

PROLOGUE

If civilisation had a dashboard, the engine warning light would be on and the engine would be making a worrying noise. People feel more offended, more exhausted, and more certain than ever that everyone else is the problem. This book starts from a ruder suspicion. At least some of the time, the problem is you, and the problem is also the author. Not because either of us are evil, but because both of us are perfectly capable of being more than a little craven with unrelenting narcissistic tendencies or in other words a CUNT.

To make that easier to spot, here are the Ten Precepts of Cunthood, the unofficial moral code of the age. You will recognise some of them in other people. The uncomfortable moment is when you recognise them in yourself.

1. **Thou shalt always put thy own convenience, comfort and feelings first.**
    Your time matters; other people do not. Your needs are urgent; other people's are optional. The universe is essentially a customer service line for you.

2. **Thou shalt treat every rule as a weapon on others and a technicality on thyself.**
   Parking rules, by-laws, policies and procedures are holy scripture when someone else breaches them, and meaningless red tape when they get in your way.

3. **Thou shalt never let ignorance, context or intention get in the way of righteous outrage.**
   You have seen one sentence, one clip, one screenshot. That is enough. Why ask a clarifying question when you can be furious right now?

4. **Thou shalt consider every 'no' an attack on thy rights, thy mental health and thy personal brand.**
   Boundaries are for other people. Any time someone declines, disagrees or does not prioritise you, they are toxic, abusive or at the very least 'not supportive of your journey'.

5. **Thou shalt confuse being offended with harm, and disagreement with oppression.**
   Discomfort is violence. Different opinions are abuse. The slightest challenge justifies maximum moral firepower.

6. **Thou shalt demand free speech for thyself, and swift punishment for those who say things thou dislike.**
   Your bluntness is 'telling it like it is'. Other people's bluntness is hate speech, bullying or grounds for sacking.

7. **Thou shalt use forms, policies and procedures to avoid responsibility while pretending to uphold standards.**
   When something goes wrong, you point at the process. You did everything 'by the book', even if the book is stupid and a human being just got eviscerated for it.

8. **Thou shalt turn every conflict, tragedy and relationship into content for thine audience.**

    Arguments, illnesses, break-ups and breakdowns are not private; they are material. The more dramatic the moment, the better it plays on your feed.

9. **Thou shalt punch down at the powerless while claiming to speak truth to power.**

    It is safer to unload on the junior staff member, the casual, the neighbour or the receptionist than on the people who actually make the rules, so that is where your courage tends to show up.

10. **Thou shalt never ask, 'What if everyone behaved like this?'**

    That question is dangerous. It turns isolated incidents into patterns, and patterns into a picture of what you are doing to the world around you. Better not to ask.

INTRODUCTION

Congratulations, you might be a cunt.

Not in the lazy way the word gets hurled out of car windows or spat across social media. Not in the affectionate Australian sense of 'he's a sick cunt', said about someone you actually like. In the quieter, more ordinary sense, it's the person who leaves a trail of bruised people and broken trust, then wonders why everyone else is so sensitive. This is not written from some enlightened, saintly perch. It is written from the muck, by someone who has, more than once, been absolutely certain they were right while behaving like a cunt.

Picture this.

It is 10:47 pm on a Tuesday. You are sitting on your couch staring at your laptop, jaw clenched, rereading an email from a work colleague who has clearly wronged you. They are ignorant, arrogant, unfair; they have cc'd the entire office into the email and are obviously the problem. You begin to type. You summon every policy, every clause, every scrap of moral high ground you can stand on. You do not write an email; you build a guided missile. Then you hit send.

For a few minutes you feel righteous, cleansed, triumphant. Then the replies begin. People are 'concerned about your tone'. You are suddenly 'verging on bullying and harassment'. Others simply stop engaging. Something in the room has shifted, and not in your favour. You may have been right on the facts, but in that moment, you were also, undeniably, a cunt.

The story that follows is one of mine.

In early May 2018, I was a volunteer general manager of a rugby federation in a developing nation. For months I had been neck-deep in organising an international tournament: logistics, officials, sponsorship, TV coverage, the works. On paper, it was a triumph. Inside, I was cooked.

The federation chairman, meanwhile, had done almost nothing. In a small federation, every hand is required to be on deck, especially from the man who bragged about his 'political connections' that could get anything done. He floated in for photos, meetings and handshakes, then floated out again. When the cameras were on, he was front and centre. When there was actual work to be done, he was nowhere. His absence, his lack of professionalism and his eagerness to take credit had been grinding on me for months.

It finally snapped over something small. Having already recovered every cent he had personally put into the tournament, he refused to pay a five-hundred-dollar hotel bill from a trip I had taken to represent the federation at a regional meeting. I had secured corporate sponsorship and was contractually entitled to a finder's fee worth about five times that bill. I had waived the fee and rolled the money back into the tournament out of good will. Faced with his flat refusal to cover my modest expense, that small invoice became my line in the sand.

So, after the tournament ended and the dust settled, I did what so many reasonable people do: I wrote the email. A beautifully crafted, deliberately remorseless email outlining his unprofessionalism and his unfitness to lead. I told him he had no strategy and no vision, that for more than twenty-two years he had presided over mediocrity and achieved very little. I reread it, admired it, felt the righteousness burning in my chest, hesitated for a heartbeat, then hit send. Whatever will be, will be.

Later, the federation's director of rugby, an Englishman and a mate, told me what happened in the office when it landed. As soon as the chairman opened it, he went off like a grenade, yelling about how unprofessional, vindictive and outrageous I was. In his story, I was the cunt. In my story, he was. The truth, as usual, sat in the messy middle. I was right on the facts. I had every reason to be angry. I was also, at that moment, a righteous cunt. And if you are honest, you probably recognise some version of that moment in yourself.

This book is about that fork in the road. The point where you can either stand on your rights, your outrage, your tribe, your technical correctness, or choose not to be a cunt. It is a book about ethics, empathy and civic responsibility, written in plain language, not a pastel-covered self-help cuddle. There are no crystals, no affirmations and no promises that you are already perfect. You are not. Neither is the author.

To see how we arrived here, you need to notice the water we have been swimming in for the last thirty years or so. In that time, greed stopped being shameful and started getting dressed up as 'ambition', 'hustle' and 'maximising your potential'. The person who takes as much as they can, from whoever they can, is no longer a villain; they are a business case study.

Over the same period, social media gave birth to the entitled influencer, whose entire existence is a rolling broadcast of 'me, my needs, my feelings, my brand'. Breakfast, breakup, breakdown and backlash all become content. The more everything is about 'my journey' and 'my truth', the easier it is to forget that other people are not extras in your personal highlight reel; they are human beings with their own lives, limits and needs.

Outrage became entertainment and a shortcut to moral status. Being furious, publicly and repeatedly, signals that you are awake and on the right side, even if you are screaming at a stranger you know nothing about. Entire platforms now reward whoever can be the loudest, the harshest, the most permanently offended.

At the same time, what you can say, and how you can say it, has been squeezed from both sides. Formally, there are hate speech laws, discrimination acts, codes of conduct, HR policies, regulations and complaints processes. Informally, there are pile-ons, call-outs, whisper networks, cancellations and reputational gulags.

Finally, the politicians who were meant to represent us stopped behaving like statesmen and stateswomen with a vision for their country and a duty to the people who put them there. Instead of making hard choices in the long-term interests of their citizens, they signed up to a hollow globalist script, deregulated and 'freed' markets, and learned to trade in slogans and outrage instead of service to the common good. In the end, we slipped further away from statehood and headfirst into cunthood.

The result is not a kinder world. It is a more anxious one. People do not become better; they become quieter. They stop saying what they think and start seething instead. They learn to smile in public and punish in private.

This book lives in the middle of that mess. It is not here to join another tribe, invent another label or hand permanent villain status to one side of politics, one generation or one identity group. The promise is simpler. You will see patterns, not just enemies, named and dissected. The same selfish, cowardly or cruel behaviour will be called out, whether it turns up in a CEO, a 'Karen', an activist, a bureaucrat or a bloke at the pub. No side is spared. If the shoe fits, it will be described in painful detail.

By the book's end, we will hopefully have landed on some kind of version of 'how not to be a cunt'. Because being less of a cunt is the only way a half-decent society keeps functioning. The behaviours described in these pages evict people, humiliate staff, blow up families, wreck workplaces, poison communities and make everyone a little more afraid of each other. A soft, soothing vocabulary has not fixed them. A sharper one might at least make them easier to see.

If you have read this far, scratching your head, unable to think of anyone who fits these descriptions, it might be time to look in the mirror and ask, as honestly as you can, 'Is it me? Am I a cunt?'

1

SO WHAT IS A CUNT, EXACTLY?

'Cunt' is a versatile word. Those four letters carry very different weights in different places. In Australia, it can mean a mate, a legend, a clown, a bastard, a stranger or a brother, sometimes all in the same sentence. Somehow, it manages to be both a chargeable offence and a backhanded compliment in the same breath. You can be a 'sick cunt' one minute and a 'shit cunt' the next. In some pubs, it is basically punctuation.

In the United States, it is treated as one of the worst things you can call someone, heavily gendered and often heard as outright misogyny, so when it appears in public, people tend to flinch. In the UK, it is still highly offensive, but it turns up more often in bloke-to-bloke insults and rough banter, sometimes with a less obvious gender sting, sometimes with all of it.

Across the English-speaking world, people argue bitterly about how offensive the word is, but this book is not about that argument. It is not a linguistics lesson and it is not a campaign to reclaim a slur. In this book, it has very little to do with anatomy and almost everything to do with being craven with unrelenting narcissistic tendencies. It is about a pattern of behaviour that quietly wrecks lives and institutions, whether or not anyone actually says the word out loud.

THE DEFINITION OF A CUNT

To fully appreciate what I mean, we must first make a historical pilgrimage into the word's etymology. The vast majority of dictionaries still define 'cunt' as 'the female genital organs'. Once upon a time, it was a blunt, working-class word for a female body part. In medieval England, you could even find it on street signs. There really was, for example, a 'Gropecunte Lane' in London, a red-light district whose name told you exactly what was on offer. People were not subtle. If you were heading to Gropecunte Lane, you were not buying bread.

The word likely has old Germanic roots, a cousin of terms in other languages, such as the Latin *cunnus*, which simply meant the vulva. For a long time, it would appear in poems, medical texts and jokes without anybody reaching for the smelling salts. Over centuries, as public prudery grew and women's bodies became more taboo, it slid from blunt descriptor to 'the unsayable C-word', the thing polite people only hint at.

By the twentieth century, its meaning had split in two. One strand is a hidden anatomical term, the other is a character insult meaning a contemptible person. It is that second strand that this book leans into. The concern here is not what people have between their legs, but what they choose to do with the power between their ears.

So what does it mean in this context? For the purposes of this book, it is someone who routinely chooses self-importance, entitlement or tribal loyalty over fairness, honesty and empathy, even when they know better. It is the person who will happily torch a relationship, a reputation or a community, then insist they are 'just telling the truth' or 'just following the rules'.

Everyone has bad days. Everyone snaps, sulks, gossips, cuts a corner or says something they regret. That is called being human. The occasional outburst does not make you a monster; it just makes you a bit of an arsehole for an afternoon. If this book tried to treat every human flaw as a hanging offence, it would be unbearable. It is not interested in the one-off blow-up but the pattern.

An ordinary arsehole loses their temper, then later feels shaky and a bit ashamed. The cunt feels satisfied and justified. An ordinary arsehole occasionally puts themselves first and later worries if they were selfish. The cunt treats other people's needs as background noise unless they interfere with their plans. An ordinary arsehole might weaponise a rule once in a blue moon. The cunt does it so often they can quote policy numbers from memory.

At the core of cunthood lies fear. Not the jump-scare sort you experience while watching a horror movie, but the deep, steady kind that hums underneath everything. Fear of being small, unseen, unimportant. The cunt doesn't lash out because they're confident; they lash out because control feels safer than connection. Every sneer, every condescending rule quote, every 'just doing my job' is a small prayer to the god of self-preservation.

Fear is the engine under the bonnet. It's what makes the cunt micromanage, hover, nitpick, and correct. It whispers that fairness is weakness, that generosity invites betrayal, that if they don't win, they'll vanish. They build little fortresses out of procedure and plausible deniability, convinced that if they can just keep everyone slightly off balance, they'll never have to feel that original smallness again. They mistake domination for competence and distance for respect. The great joke, of course, is that the thing they fear most, being exposed as ordinary, is written all over them.

Some cunts can be wildly charming. They are brilliant at dinner parties and funerals. They tell great stories, raise money for charity and cry in the right places. They may be much loved by the people above them and quietly feared by the people below them. None of that matters if, when decisions are made and power is used, the default setting is 'me and mine first, everyone else is expendable'. You have probably worked with one. You may have been raised by one. On certain days, if you are very honest, you may be one.

THE THREE PILLARS OF CUNTHOOD

The behaviour that matters here usually leans on three pillars. On their own, each pillar is just a bad habit. Combined, they build something much nastier.

Entitlement

The first pillar is entitlement. Entitlement means 'my time, my feelings, my beliefs and my comfort matter more than yours, by default'. It shows up when you believe rules are there to protect you, not apply to you. It shows up when you expect exceptional treatment as standard and experience any limit or boundary as an insult. In that mindset, everyone else is a support act whose job is not to be inconvenient.

Cowardice

The second pillar is cowardice. Cowardice here is not fear itself, but the choice to protect yourself at other people's expense, especially when you have some power. It shows up when you complain to everyone except the person who could actually fix the problem, when you copy half the organisation into your 'concerns' instead of speaking privately, when you hide behind committees, processes and 'we' language so no one can pin responsibility on you. You do not swing the axe yourself; you just 'regret to advise' that the axe has fallen.

Cruelty

The third pillar is cruelty. Cruelty is the willingness to hurt, humiliate or frighten people and then blame them for feeling it. It shows up when you share something knowing it will ruin someone's reputation and feel a secret thrill. It shows up when you use jokes to belittle and then accuse people of having 'no sense of humour' when they flinch. It shows up when you deliberately press on people's weak spots to win a point or a power struggle, then tell yourself they are just 'too sensitive'.

FAMILIAR FACES

You do not have to be loud to hit all three pillars. You can be polite, well-spoken, educated, softly spoken and still behave this way if you consistently take more than your share, hide behind process instead of owning your choices and enjoy watching people squirm when you have them cornered.

To make this less abstract, picture a few familiar faces:

- The politician who promises an open and transparent government, unlike their predecessors, then buries everything behind 'cabinet in confidence' and 'ongoing investigation' and shuts the door on any real access to information.

- The business owner who talks a big game about performance reviews, salary increases and career progression, then quietly loads people up with more work and never delivers on a single promise.
- The corporate manager who launches a 'zero-tolerance' bullying policy with a PowerPoint and a smile, then spends their days undermining staff behind closed doors and punishing anyone who dares to call it what it is.
- The strata committee president who blocks urgent repairs to an elderly neighbour's apartment, then quietly signs off on contractors to spruce up their own lot at the corporation's expense, and still turns up to meetings to lecture everyone else about 'doing the right thing'.
- The social activist who talks endlessly about compassion and justice online, but delights in public shaming and pile-ons, and never checks whether what they are sharing is actually true.
- The neighbour who demands absolute silence from everyone else but uses power tools on a Sunday because 'it's my property and I pay rates'.

None of these people would describe themselves as villains. Many of them see themselves as principled, even brave. That is part of the problem.

In the current climate, people often treat their level of offence as the only moral gauge that matters. Being offended becomes the trump card that ends the conversation. If that is the standard, then almost everyone is a villain to someone, all the time, simply for existing in public. As a way of working out how to live together, getting upset is useless.

Adults upset one another all the time. The more useful questions are whether they lied about you or misrepresented you in order to win, whether they abused their power over you, knowing you had less ability to push back, whether they deliberately humiliated you in front of others, whether they treated you as less than fully human because it served their ego, tribe or comfort.

If the answer is yes, you have probably encountered the kind of behaviour this book is interested in. If the answer is no, you may simply have met another adult with a different opinion, a different style. Or maybe they were having a bad day. You are allowed to be uncomfortable. You are allowed to be challenged, offended, even angry. That does not automatically mean the other person has done this particular kind of damage.

THE SOCIAL CONTRACT

Every society runs on a kind of unspoken deal, a social contract, if you will. You do not always get the opportunity to negotiate the terms, nor do you sign it or get a copy in the mail, but you live inside it every day. It says, more or less, that you will not drive like a maniac even though your car can, that you will queue even though you could push in, that you will pay your share even though you could probably dodge it, that you will tell the truth often enough that people can trust your word, and that you will use your little patch of power without terrorising everyone under you.

In return, you expect other people to do the same. You expect teachers not to abuse students, police not to frame suspects, bosses not to steal wages, husbands not to abuse wives, drug dealers not to sell to children, neighbours not to turn the street into a war zone. None of this is guaranteed. It holds only because enough people, enough of the time, decide to act as if other human beings matter.

That is the fragile social contract.

As a society, we may wrap ourselves in laws, regulations and guidelines, but the real contract is not a law book and it is not a political theory text. It is millions of tiny, boring acts of restraint and decency that make it possible for strangers to live together without constant fear.

Cunthood is a decision to quietly tear up your side of that contract while still demanding everyone else keep theirs. You drive like the rules do not apply to you but lose your mind when someone cuts you off. You underpay staff or gouge clients but talk loudly about 'people doing the right thing'. You file complaints, pull strings or use connections to get your way, then rant about 'corruption' when others do the same.

Every time you do that, you send a signal that the game is rigged and only suckers play fair.

The more people receive that message, the more they begin to cheat, lie, withdraw or harden in self-defence. Trust dies first, then cooperation, then any sense that we share a future.

Ethics can get complicated quickly if you let it. You do not need a philosophy degree to use one simple test. What would this place look like if everyone behaved like this? Take almost any situation in your life and run it through that lens. If everyone sent the nuclear email instead of walking down the hall, how long before nobody trusted 'reply all' again? If everyone lodged weaponised complaints instead of having hard conversations, how long before every workplace became paralysed by fear?

If everyone chased every dollar they could wring out of the system and left the mess to someone else, how long before the system collapsed under the weight of rorts? If everyone treated strangers as content, staff as props and rules as weapons, how long before basic decency felt like a rare personality disorder? If the honest answer is that this home, this office, this building or this country would become unliveable very quickly, then you are not looking at a harmless quirk. You are looking at behaviour that, multiplied by millions, quietly murders trust and civility.

If you want to see what it looks like when that process runs to the end of the line, you do not have to imagine a dystopian novel. You can look at a real country that spent decades quietly tearing up its social contract until almost nothing was left holding it together.

THE PARIS OF THE MIDDLE EAST — OR SO THEY SAID

Lebanon used to be marketed as the 'Paris of the Middle East', a small coastal country on the eastern shores of the Mediterranean, with a glamorous capital, a service-heavy economy and a reputation for nightlife, banks and beaches. On paper it was a cosmopolitan playground. Underneath, it rested on a fragile bargain: sectarian power-sharing between rival religious and political factions, foreign interests quietly tilting the table, money washing in from the region and the diaspora, and a banking system selling the fantasy of stability and generous returns. The whole thing only held together for as long as enough people agreed to pretend the game was fair.

From 1975 to 1990, Lebanon's civil war destroyed buildings, killed people and shredded basic trust in the state as a neutral referee. Public services such as electricity, water, healthcare and education deteriorated so badly that non-state actors, sectarian parties, militias and local bosses stepped in to fill the gaps, each 'looking after their own' in return for loyalty. When the war formally ended, many of the same warlords and militia leaders simply swapped fatigues for suits and moved into government, bringing their client networks with them. Instead of rebuilding a state that treated citizens equally, the postwar order entrenched patronage and corruption as the price of getting anything done.

Over the next three decades, that corruption and short-term self-interest hollowed out Lebanon's economy and institutions. Successive governments borrowed heavily, ran up unsustainable public debt and relied on remittances from expatriates and foreign currency inflows to prop up a fixed exchange rate that made the banking system look magically stable. Key institutions, from the central bank to regulatory agencies, were treated as tools of sectarian and personal power. The social contract thinned out into a kind of shared delusion: you hand over taxes, deposits and votes, and in return you get...vibes.

The National Army was kept deliberately underfunded and under-equipped, while a foreign-backed militia accumulated weapons, set red lines, determined foreign policy, and periodically dragged the country into regional conflicts it had not chosen and could not afford, on behalf of interests that were, to put it generously, not Lebanon's. The 'contract' became one-sided: citizens were expected to tolerate failing services, inequality and arbitrary enforcement while the political class and their armed partners siphoned off resources and faced almost no consequences. The state kept the letterhead; everyone else kept the guns and the money.

By late 2019, the façade cracked. The Lebanese pound went into freefall, eventually losing most of its value. Prices for basics soared. Banks imposed informal capital controls that trapped people's life savings. Fuel shortages produced crippling blackouts, with many homes getting only a few hours of electricity a day. Jobs vanished, businesses closed and a large share of the population was pushed into poverty. Outside observers described the economic collapse as one of the worst crises anywhere in the world since the nineteenth century. For ordinary people, it felt like their country had simply stopped working – the social contract repossessed overnight.

Then, on 4 August 2020, came the moment that turned the metaphor into twisted metal and glass. In a warehouse at the Port of Beirut, thousands of tonnes of ammonium nitrate had been stored unsafely for years. From the president down to the lowliest customs official at the port, everyone knew it was there. Warnings had been sent, reports filed, responsibilities shuffled from one office to another. No-one with the power to fix it did the boring, necessary thing. A fire in the hangar triggered a detonation big enough to be heard in another country, one of the largest non-nuclear explosions in human history. It killed more than two hundred people, injured thousands, displaced hundreds of thousands and shredded large parts of a city that was already on its knees.

The blast investigation revealed what many Lebanese already knew: multiple arms of the state had known about the danger and left it sitting there anyway, each pointing to paperwork and someone else's desk. That is what a dead social contract looks like up close. A state that cannot reliably provide electricity or safe drinking water. A banking system that devours its citizens' savings. A political class so entangled in its own impunity and mutual protection that it leaves a city sitting on a floating mine of fertiliser until it explodes. The message was simple: your lives are negotiable; our comfort is not.

And even that was not the end of the story.

Years after the economic collapse and the port explosion, Lebanon remained trapped in the same structural weakness: a state that formally governs the country but does not fully control its own territory, its own foreign policy or its own war and peace. When Israel and the United States struck targets in Iran in February 2026, they did so against the backdrop of a ceasefire with Lebanon that Israel itself had already treated less as a binding agreement than as a flexible suggestion, violating it repeatedly in the name of 'security'. In that steadily eroding framework, Hezbollah – supposedly bound by the November 2024 ceasefire that followed the near-total destruction of its senior leadership, military and financial apparatus – decided it still had one more war left in it.

From southern Lebanon and south Beirut, the militia group unilaterally launched rockets into Israel, acting without the consent of the Lebanese government or the Lebanese Armed Forces, as if national policy were just another private militia portfolio to be managed off-balance-sheet. In effect, a non-state actor made a sovereign decision on war and peace and dragged an exhausted country back to the brink. Whatever was left of the social contract – the basic understanding that only the state decides on war in the name of all its citizens – was treated as optional fine print.

The irony is that this solo act of "resistance" finally turned the tide of Lebanese opinion against Hezbollah. As more than 1,000,000 people were driven from their homes in southern Lebanon and Beirut's southern suburbs, families once willing to tolerate the "armed wing" as the price of stability now found themselves packing suitcases in the dark for yet another round of displacement. The supposed shield of the nation had become the wrecking ball of whatever remained of its social contract. Israel's earlier breaches and Hezbollah's latest gambit met, as usual, in the living rooms and bank accounts of people who had no say in either decision.

For years, Lebanon's fragile bargain had been an unspoken one: the state pretends it governs, Hezbollah pretends it consults, Israel pretends the ceasefire is elastic, and ordinary people pretend this arrangement isn't slowly hollowing out their future. This time, the pretence snapped. The President and Prime Minister took the unprecedented step of formally instructing the army to arrest any armed Hezbollah member, effectively declaring that the group's guns no longer enjoyed even the fiction of state approval. A militia that had long claimed to defend the country now found itself, on paper at least, on the wrong side of its laws

– another crack in a contract that no one was honouring but everyone was paying for.

The consequences for ordinary Lebanese were immediate and familiar. Tens, then hundreds of thousands of civilians in southern Lebanon and Beirut's southern suburbs were forced to evacuate their homes as the border region became an active battlefield again and the possibility of a wider invasion hung in the air. A country already crippled by economic collapse suddenly found itself staring down another regional conflict it had neither voted for nor prepared for. Once again, the fine print read: you will bear the costs of other people's calculations.

This is what happens when the monopoly on violence, the basic foundation of any functioning state, fractures. War becomes something that can be triggered by factions, patrons and regional alliances rather than by the institutions meant to represent the population as a whole. The people who suffer the consequences are almost never the ones who made the decision. Lebanon did not fall apart because one person was a spectacular cunt on a bad day. It fell apart because, over decades, enough people with power – at home and abroad – chose entitlement, cowardice and cruelty over their side of the bargain, until the basic conditions for trust and safety were gone.

When you scale up everyday cunthood – rules for you, exemptions for me; loyalty to my group, indifference to yours; process as a shield instead of a responsibility – it does not just make one workplace toxic or one building unliveable. It can turn a place that once sold itself as the 'Paris of the Middle East' into somewhere people flee because the lights fail, the money is worthless and the institutions are dangerous. The social contract doesn't collapse all at once; it frays, excuse by excuse, exemption by exemption, until one day you look up and realise the only thing still working on schedule is the next disaster.

Most countries are not Lebanon, and most buildings are not ports sitting on tonnes of explosives. But the mechanism is the same, whether it is a body corporate, a business, a school, a council or a nation. Every time someone tears up their side of the social contract while demanding everyone else keep theirs, the place becomes a little bit less liveable for everyone. Do it long enough, and you don't just lose services or money. You lose the basic belief that the system is for you at all – and once that goes, it is very hard to get back.

THE MIRROR

You probably already have a mental slideshow running. The chairman, the boss, the ex, the neighbour, the committee, the influencer, the politician. Keep them. Some of them will show up, lightly disguised, in later chapters.

But here is the more uncomfortable thing. The time you loved being technically right more than you cared about being fair. The time you let someone smaller take the hit so you didn't have to admit a mistake. The time you piled on, or stayed silent, because it was safer than asking whether what was happening was actually fair.

That shape. You recognise it.

2

HISTORICAL CUNTS

If you want to understand why this behaviour matters, you don't start with Hitler, Stalin or Mao. You start with the neighbour next door, the chairperson, the boss, the bureaucrat. You start small, because that's where it lives most of the time: in car parks and meetings and email chains, not in Nuremberg rallies. But if you want to see what happens when entitlement, cowardice and cruelty are handed armies, secret police and a national branding kit, sooner or later you have to talk about the twentieth century.

The three cunts we're about to meet are not the only historical cunts worth mentioning. Sadly, history is basically a highlight reel of cunts with good timing and bad morals. There's a whole litany of them: Attila the Hun, Genghis Khan, Ivan the Terrible of Russia, Leopold II of Belgium, Pol Pot and the list goes on and on. I've picked three of the most prominent operators who, in the space of half a century, directly and indirectly managed to stack up bodies in the tens of millions.

THE CUNT WITH A DESTINY — ADOLF HITLER

Adolf Hitler did not invent hatred, humiliation or conspiracy theories. Germany after the First World War was already a mess: hyperinflation, mass unemployment, sexual depravity, political street fights and wounded pride. He just offered a story that gathered all that pain and pointed it like a weapon. In his story, 'proper' Germans were entitled to reclaim greatness, and almost everyone who got in the way, such as Jews, Marxists, foreigners, the disabled, homosexuals and 'degenerates', was secretly plotting to destroy them.

Hitler built a cult of personality with rallies, uniforms, slogans and carefully staged images of himself as the tireless, infallible Führer. He sold people a version of themselves that centred around being strong, pure, wronged, destined. That is entitlement on a national scale, not 'I deserve a pay rise', but 'we deserve living space, resources, domination, and your existence is negotiable if it helps us get there'.

His cowardice was dressed as strength. Instead of facing the messiness of modern life, he offered simple, magical answers. Purge the 'parasites', ignore international law, crush opposition, burn the evidence. When reality pushed back, he doubled down, lashed out and took a whole country with him.

And then there was the cruelty. Not just the headline horror of gas chambers and mass shootings, but the systematic humiliation. Jews forced to scrub streets, families herded into ghettos, disabled people sterilised or killed under euthanasia programs, all wrapped in bureaucratic paperwork and medical language. It was cunthood in its purest form. Strip a group of their humanity, call it necessary and sleep like a baby.

Most Germans did not personally shoot anyone in a ditch. They filled forms, drove trains, stamped permits, hung flags, kept their heads down and told themselves they had no choice. That is how one man's pathology becomes everyone's normal.

How a Whole Nation Becomes Cunts

A whole nation didn't wake up one morning and decide to become cunts. It slid there, bit by bit, through fear, flattery, convenience and a thousand small abdications of responsibility. Most Germans did not become card-carrying sadists. What they did buy into was a story that explained their pain, defeat, humiliation and unemployment, and gave them someone to blame and punish.

They enjoyed the early pay-offs: jobs, orderly streets, national pride. They decided, quietly, that their own family's safety and prosperity mattered more than the fate of neighbours who were a tiny minority and constantly demonised. By the mid-1930s, the regime was wildly popular. Many had at least a vague idea that minority groups were being persecuted. They might not have pictured death camps or SS extermination squads, but they saw the boycotts, the smashed shop windows, the colleagues who stopped coming to work. They accepted the isolation, dispossession and violence along the way.

After the war, psychologists started asking an awkward question. How much pressure does it actually take to get ordinary people to do horrible things? Here were some observations:

- In obedience experiments, most participants were willing to deliver what they believed were dangerous electric shocks to a stranger because a calm man in a lab coat told them to carry on. Many described themselves as feeling like 'agents' of the authority, not responsible for what they were doing.
- In mock prison experiments, volunteers randomly assigned as 'guards' quickly became more dominant and aggressive, especially when told that toughness was necessary.

- In bystander studies, people were far less likely to intervene in an emergency when others were present, assuming someone else would act or that the situation wasn't really their business.

Scale that up to a country. Respected authorities wearing uniforms instead of lab coats. Everyone around you is complying. Victims defined as dangerous, dirty or less than fully human. In that environment, it actually takes more courage and imagination *not* to be a cunt.

Nations don't become cunty overnight; they are trained. Propaganda recasts cruelty as necessity and kindness as weakness. Law and policy slowly redefine who counts as 'us' and who is disposable. Rewards and punishments teach you what gets you ahead and what ruins your life.

Join the party, look away, take the flat or job of the family that 'moved'; or, on the other side, speak up and lose everything. By the time the worst crimes are being committed, most people are not cheering for mass murder. They are hooked into a system where *not* going along feels suicidal, and where backing away from the truth becomes a habit.

BEFORE JOSEPH STALIN – THE BOLSHEVIK TEMPLATE

To understand Joseph Stalin, you have to meet the cunts who warmed up his seat for him. The Bolsheviks did not stumble on terror by accident. From the beginning, they preached a gospel in which their vision of history justified almost any violence against class enemies. Within months of taking power in 1917, they launched what became known as the Red Terror, a campaign of arrests, executions and camps aimed at wiping out real and imagined opponents.

They shot political rivals, industrialists, landowners and anyone unlucky enough to be labelled 'counter-revolutionary'. In places like

Crimea, surrendered prisoners and civilians were lined up and killed despite promises of amnesty. The message was simple: the revolution is pure, you are dirt, and dirt gets swept away.

They literally murdered the entire Russian royal family to make the point. In July 1918, as civil war raged, Bolshevik secret police woke the Romanovs in the middle of the night, marched them to a basement in Yekaterinburg and shot and bayoneted the tsar, his wife, their five children and the loyal staff who happened to be with them. No trial, no pretence, just a bullet-pointed lesson: there will be no going back, and no one is too symbolic, too innocent or too royal to kill.

The church did not fare much better. Bolshevik ideology treated religion as an enemy of progress and the Orthodox clergy as a class to be broken. Priests, monks and nuns were arrested, tortured and executed in their thousands during the early 1920s. Church property was seized, monasteries dissolved, thousands of churches shut or demolished. By the late 1930s, only a tiny fraction of pre-revolutionary parishes were still open. Officially, this was all 'hypermoral' work, necessary cleansing for a just society. In reality, it trained a generation to see terror as normal politics, fellow citizens as raw material and law as a weapon, not a restraint.

When the smoke of the civil war cleared and the Red Terror ended, an estimated one to two million Russians had been killed with estimates as high as between seven to twelve million dying throughout the conflict from widespread disease, starvation, massacres by both sides, and pogroms against Jews. By the time of Stalin's ascent, Russia had already executed a deposed royal family in a cellar, conducted en masse campaigns against class enemies and believers, and normalised secret police, prison camps and rule by decree. The system had decided that some lives did not count, that killing for the cause was virtuous, and that God, kings and conscience were obstacles to be bulldozed. Stalin did not invent that. He grew up moulded by it.

THE PARANOID BOOKKEEPER OF SOULS – JOSEPH STALIN

Joseph Stalin wrapped his cunthood in the language of equality and workers' liberation. In theory, the Soviet Union was the vanguard of justice, while in practice, ordinary people were fed into a meat grinder powered by paranoia and concrete. He took the tools the early Bolsheviks had already tested – the security police, the habit of 'mass terror', the contempt for independent churches and courts – and turned up the dial until it snapped off.

His entitlement said, 'I and the party know what is necessary, and any life, law or fact that gets in the way can be bent, erased or buried.' Peasants resisting collectivisation were branded kulaks, enemies of the people. Their land was seized, grain requisitioned and entire regions starved into submission in man-made famines. Millions died, not because there was no food, but because the state decided other priorities mattered more.

Stalin's cowardice showed up as permanent purging. He was terrified of rivals, criticism and reality itself. Instead of facing weaknesses in the system, he invented plots, doctors' conspiracies, spies under every bed, traitors in every ministry. The Great Purge swallowed party officials, military officers, intellectuals, ordinary citizens – anyone unlucky enough to be denounced, misquoted or simply standing near the wrong person. Admitting error would have meant stepping into the crosshairs himself. So the show trials rolled on and the prisons filled.

His cruelty was industrial. The Gulag, that archipelago of labour camps across the Soviet Union, turned millions of people into disposable tools. Prisoners froze, starved, broke and died building canals, railways and mines that no one will remember their names for. Families were notified in dead phrases: ten years, no right of correspondence. People vanished into a paperwork hole.

Again, the machine depended on layers of small cunthoods – local officials lying to meet impossible quotas, informants denouncing neighbours out of fear, jealousy or convenience, guards who could see exactly what was happening and told themselves they were just doing their jobs. No single person invented the Gulag. It was the sum of millions of small decisions to protect themselves at someone else's expense.

Stalin did not turn a peaceful, law-abiding country into a nightmare all by himself. He inherited a system that had already decided terror was acceptable and then proved how far you could push that logic if you stripped away the last restraints. He was not the first cunt through the door. He was just the one who slammed it behind him and threw away the key.

THE REVOLUTIONARY EMPEROR – MAO ZEDONG

Mao Zedong managed a kind of greatest hits compilation of ideological cunthood. He genuinely believed in revolution, but he also believed in his own genius so absolutely that dissent became treason and data became optional.

The Great Leap Off a Cliff

When Mao launched the Great Leap Forward in 1958, the pitch was simple and deranged: China would rocket past its capitalist rivals by sheer willpower. Backyard furnaces would churn out steel, peasants in vast communes would smash production records and the new communist man would conquer nature itself. It was the political equivalent of deciding you'll get rich by burning your house for warmth and calling it 'energy innovation'.

Villages melted down pots, pans and farm tools to meet insane steel quotas, producing useless lumps of pig iron while the real tools that actually grew food disappeared. Officials ordered 'close planting' and other crackpot methods that wrecked yields, then lied through their teeth about bumper harvests to prove their loyalty. On paper, the fields were overflowing. In reality, grain rotted in state granaries or was shipped abroad to keep up appearances, while the people who grew it starved.

Best estimates put the death toll from the famine somewhere in the tens of millions. This was not a bad season. This was a slow-motion massacre caused by policies that diverted labour from agriculture, demanded impossible procurements and punished anyone who told the truth. Mao's entitlement said, 'My vision is worth your children's lives.' His cowardice refused to admit disaster, even as reports of mass starvation piled up. His cruelty lay in the insistence on maintaining high grain exports and revolutionary bragging rights while peasants were literally eating bark and mud.

If you want a tidy definition of scaled-up cunthood, it is this: millions of preventable deaths dismissed as the necessary cost of a political story you are too proud to abandon.

The Cult and the Kids with Sticks

You might hope that after presiding over the worst famine in recorded human history, a leader would be hustled into retirement and given a gardening column. Mao did the opposite. Threatened by more pragmatic colleagues and stung by criticism, he decided the real problem was that people were not revolutionary enough, so he turned the country's teenagers into a weapon.

During the Cultural Revolution, Mao's face was everywhere. Huge portraits, badges and, above all, the Little Red Book of quotations that every citizen was expected to carry and chant from. He cultivated a personality cult, reasoning that Khrushchev had fallen in the USSR because he lacked one. If the party or reality pushed back, Mao could simply bypass them by appealing directly to 'the masses', and the masses he loved most were the young and volatile ones.

The Red Guards were unleashed with slogans like 'to rebel is justified', told to smash the 'Four Olds' – old ideas, culture, customs, habits – and hunt down 'bourgeois' enemies wherever they lurked. In practice, this meant teachers and principals were beaten by their own students, sometimes to death. Intellectuals paraded in dunce caps, heads shaved, forced to confess imaginary crimes while being kicked and spat on. Homes were ransacked, temples and ancestral halls destroyed, books burned, people assaulted in the street for having the wrong clothes or the wrong haircut.

At one point, Beijing issued an order forbidding police from intervening in Red Guard activities, and officers who tried were branded 'counter-revolutionaries'. Mao praised 'great disorder under heaven' as a sign that things were, in his words, 'excellent'. Translation: the violence meant his enemies were on the back foot.

Estimates vary, but roughly a million people may have died as a direct result of Cultural Revolution violence, with many more driven to suicide, prison, internal exile or mental collapse. Universities shut down for years, production slumped and whole sectors of society were traumatised or decapitated. Mao's China turned an entire generation into both victims and perpetrators. Kids were taught that loyalty meant how enthusiastically you could denounce, beat and destroy.

Again, this was not chaos by accident. It was cunthood as strategy. Mao set the tone, then allowed and encouraged local factions to escalate, only reining them in when the fire he'd lit started licking around the foundations of his own power.

The God Who Still Needed Scapegoats

Even inside the cult, Mao could not stand limits. When things spun completely out of control, he let lieutenants blame 'ultra-Leftists' or overzealous followers for 'excesses', as if he hadn't spent years cheering them on. Later, under Deng Xiaoping, the party would officially declare the Cultural Revolution a 'catastrophe' and quietly put the personality cult back in its box, but by then the damage was done.

What makes Mao such a useful case study is not just the numbers, the tens of millions dead in famine, the millions more battered by purges and campaigns. It is the clarity with which his story shows the three pillars working together:

- Entitlement – treating a nation as a laboratory, a stage and a mirror for his own revolutionary self-image.
- Cowardice – refusing to face reality, blaming saboteurs, rightists and 'capitalist roaders' whenever his schemes failed, never himself.
- Cruelty – deliberately loosening the leash on humiliation and violence, then stepping back to watch enemies, real and imagined, be torn apart in his name.

Strip away the scale and the iconography and you are left with something you already recognise from much smaller rooms: a man who cannot be wrong, who would rather watch everything burn than apologise, who teaches everyone around him that loyalty means hurting the people he hates.

The difference is that Mao got to run a fifth of humanity while he worked that out.

'MONSTERS' VERSUS 'MEN LIKE US'

It is comforting to treat Hitler, Stalin and Mao as monsters - glitches in an otherwise sensible human species. If they are monsters, we can tell ourselves we would never end up like that. We are decent people with Netflix, who only consume fairtrade organic coffee. We are safe.

The trouble is, on the surface they are wildly different. A failed artist, a Georgian seminarian, a bookish peasant revolutionary. Underneath, they are cousins - and depressingly ordinary ones at that. Petty. Vain. Thin-skinned. Obsessed with loyalty. Prone to sulking and score-settling.

All three built stories of entitlement: Hitler's racial destiny, Stalin's vanguard party, Mao's revolutionary purity. All three institutionalised cowardice: bad news could not travel upwards, honest feedback became suicide, and anyone who told the truth was branded a traitor. All three normalised cruelty as virtue: violence against the enemy was not a shameful last resort but proof of loyalty.

The difference between them and you was not that they felt different emotions. It was what they did with them, how many people believed their stories, and how few guardrails there were to stop them. They also were not alone. Their cunthood went nuclear because millions of smaller cunts - and millions more frightened, compromised, exhausted people - chose to go along for the ride.

You have felt versions of their impulses. You have wanted someone to pay for embarrassing you. You have fantasised about silencing a critic or humiliating a rival. You have been tempted to lie to save face. You have enjoyed, just a little, seeing an enemy get their comeuppance.

The gap between you and a dictator is measured in power, opportunity and how many people are willing to say no. Take away constraints, feed your worst instincts and surround yourself with people who benefit from your tantrums, and while you may not turn into a mass-murdering dictator, you might turn into a much worse version of yourself than you like to imagine.

THE BANALITY OF CUNTHOOD

One of the most chilling discoveries after the Second World War, and then again when Soviet and Chinese archives opened, was how ordinary the paperwork of mass crime looked. Requisitions, minutes, transport schedules, medical forms. Lists of names, numbers, signatures. No horns, no flames. Just the admin of hell.

The philosopher Hannah Arendt, in her account of the trial of Nazi war criminal Adolf Eichmann in Jerusalem in 1961, called it 'the banality of evil', the way horrors can be carried out not just by raving sadists but by men in suits who are more worried about their promotion prospects than the human beings on the trains they schedule. In the language of this book, you could call it 'the banality of cunthood':

- The official who knows a law is unjust but enforces it zealously because it is 'more than his job is worth' to question it.
- The officer who 'just follows orders', even when those orders involve rounding up and murdering neighbours.
- The administrator who manipulates a system to save his own skin and consigns someone else to a camp, famine or firing squad.

Every one of them had reasons. Every one of them could tell a story in which they were not the villain. Taken together, they turned cunthood from a personal failing into a system.

THE FINE LINE

Unless you are reading this from a presidential bunker, you are not going to orchestrate a genocide. You are, however, living in a time that quietly flatters some of the same instincts that made the twentieth century such a blood-soaked mess.

You will almost certainly never be in a position to order a purge. You will, however, be in situations where you can punish someone socially or professionally because they embarrassed you and you are tempted to dress it up as principle; where you can stay silent while someone weaker is being fed to the wolves because speaking up might cost you; where you can lie about the numbers, fudge the report or blame policy instead of admitting a mistake.

3

THE AGE OF ME

Humans have always been selfish, entitled and cruel. That is how empires were built and how rulers took and held power, how people were conquered and enslaved. Long before hashtags and loyalty programs, kings grabbed land because they believed God or blood gave them the right, armies burned villages so their own cities could feast and whole populations were worked to death so a handful of people could live in marble and silk.

The tools have changed, but the basic reflex – 'my comfort matters more than your suffering' – has been with us as long as we've had flags and fences. None of that is new. What is new is how ordinary that reflex can feel when an entire culture is built around the idea that life is, fundamentally, about you, your goals, your brand, your feelings, your truth.

If you're raised to believe your inner world is the main plot and everyone else is the supporting cast, the old brutal logic of 'them for us' quietly shrinks to 'them for me', and it stops feeling brutal. It just feels like common sense.

THE AGE OF WE – THE GENERATIONS THAT ATE LAST

It's easy to forget, while doom-scrolling the latest outrage, that not so long ago people were raised in a completely different moral climate. The men and women we now dismiss as dinosaurs grew up under conditions that would shatter most modern egos by Wednesday. Born roughly between 1900 and the mid-1920s, they came of age during the Depression, survived wartime rationing and, for many families, the loss or maiming of sons, brothers and fathers on foreign battlefields.

They were taught, often brutally, that you didn't eat until others were fed, that you did your duty even when nobody clapped, and that 'how you feel about it' came a distant second to what needed to be done. They did not have therapists. They did not have safe spaces. They had a shovel and a problem.

Historians call them the Greatest Generation, a label that has always carried a faint whiff of self-congratulation, but which becomes increasingly difficult to contest the longer you sit with what they actually lived through. The oldest among them did not merely grow up in the shadow of the Great War, some of them fought in it, enlisting as teenagers into a conflict that consumed entire old and new world generations.

Those who came back were so damaged in ways that had no clinical name, no treatment protocol, and no patience from a world that needed them to be fine. Those who didn't come back didn't, of course, come back at all. The younger among them grew up watching these men, their fathers, their elder brothers, their neighbours, and learned early that some things could not be spoken of, and that this was simply how life was.

Then came the Spanish flu, not a pandemic managed through briefings and furlough schemes, but a killing event that moved through populations like a fire through dry grass, taking somewhere between fifty and a hundred million people before it tired of the work. Then the Depression. Then, before the century had reached its fortieth year, another world war, larger, more systematic in its cruelties, and fought across every ocean and continent simultaneously.

They fought it. They buried their dead in foreign soil. They came home to streets that looked the same and lives that did not. And then, and this is the part that should stop us cold, they got on with it. Nobody scheduled a debrief. Nobody asked them how that made them feel. They just helped to build the modern world, raised families, paid their taxes, and tried not to think about it too much. Most of them succeeded. The ones who didn't rarely talked about it either.

Scarcity was the air they breathed, unemployment, queues for food, clothes patched and repatched, petrol and meat rationed for the war effort. Survival and sacrifice were their daily job. Out of that came a particular kind of character. You can and should criticise it for its blind spots, its silences about trauma, its stiff upper lip and its tolerance of all sorts of private misery. But you can't miss the core assumption; you are part of something bigger than yourself.

The country is at war, so you queue and ration and work long hours. Your mates are under fire, so you enlist, or you weld ships, or you build planes, or you grow food, or you keep the factories running. You don't need to enjoy it. You do it because that is what decent people do when everything is on the line. Many of them barely spoke about what they saw. They came back from fronts, factories and bombed cities and got on with building lives. They saved. They were thrifty because they knew what it was to have nothing. They believed in steady work, in paying debts, in not wasting things.

They valued loyalty, reliability, keeping your word. Their bodies carried the scars and their minds carried the nightmares, but their public posture was brutally simple: get on with it. If you tried to talk to my grandfather about 'self-care', he would have assumed you meant washing. You could watch that entire worldview coming loose at the edges as they aged. A man who had once crouched in a trench now lived in a world of wellness influencers and streaming services, being told to 'put himself first' and 'live his best life'.

A woman who had once handed over ration coupons and scrubbed other people's floors now watched grown adults complain publicly about being 'traumatised' by slow Wi-Fi. The shift wasn't just technological. It was spiritual. It came into sharp focus in one old man's expression on live television. On the eve of Remembrance Day 2025, a 100-year-old Second World War veteran sat in a British TV studio, medals on his chest, and was lobbed the usual soft question about what the day meant to him. He didn't give the standard answer about pride and gratitude.

He said that when he closed his eyes, he could still see rows and rows of white marble crosses, all the mates who never came home, and then he said, very clearly, that looking at the state of the country today, 'the sacrifice wasn't worth the result that it is now'. The presenters almost fell off their chairs. They apologised to viewers and to him on behalf of the nation, tried to reassure him that people were grateful, tried to slap on a neat line about 'our duty now'. But the sentence hung there: 'it wasn't worth it'.

You don't have to agree with his verdict to comprehend what it means. A man who lived through rationing, bombardment, war, the death of his friends and real fascism was looking at a rich peacetime country of rolling scandals, brittle politics, bad-faith arguments and performative outrage and wondering if this was really the prize. In his eyes, the freedoms he and his friends bled for have been squandered by people who treat 'freedom' as a slogan while happily bullying, censoring, humiliating and looting whenever it suits them.

Many of the loudest beneficiaries of the Age of Me who saw that clip would have written him off as a bitter old man, a dinosaur, a reactionary; in other words, a cunt for daring to suggest we might not be as noble as we like to imagine. That, in itself, says plenty about the age we're in.

Those generations had their own brutalities and hypocrisies, and plenty of people suffered in silence because 'we do not talk about those things'. But it matters that, for a large chunk of the twentieth century, the dominant story wasn't 'you are the main character; chase your bliss'. It was 'you are part of a family, a unit, a community, a nation; act like it'. Personal freedom mattered, but it sat inside a wider frame of duty and belonging.

The people who stormed the beaches of Normandy, huddled in air-raid shelters, stood in breadlines or sent their sons overseas would struggle to recognise a world in which adults throw public tantrums over coffee orders, or melt down online because a stranger disagreed with them. Not because they were better humans; many were racist, sexist, violent or emotionally frozen. But because the scale of what was at stake when they were young forced them to see themselves as one small part of a larger whole. We, by contrast, have been trained to see ourselves as the larger whole.

THE FLIP FROM 'WE' TO 'ME'

Over the next few decades, that frame flipped. The people who were told 'you are small, the cause is big, do your part' raised children and grandchildren on a very different catechism: 'you are special, follow your dreams, don't let anyone hold you back.' The classroom posters, the ads between cartoons, the guidance counsellors and the inspirational quotes all hummed the same tune. Be true to yourself, prioritise your happiness, never settle. We marinated in it.

A lot of that was a badly needed correction. Women, migrants and anyone outside the old default were no longer expected to quietly swallow whatever the 'greater good' demanded of them. Mental illness stopped being something you drank over. Speaking about abuse stopped being framed as betrayal. There is real justice in that shift, and only a fool would want to wind the clock back to the days when duty meant 'shut up and endure'.

But every gain also throws a shadow. When you grow up steeped in the idea that your feelings are sacred, your wants are urgent and your identity the main plotline, the edges of the self start to blur. Boredom, frustration and compromise feel like moral injuries rather than part of adult life. Other people's needs start to register as obstacles or background noise. That is the soil modern cunthood grows in.

Those shared standards - the unspoken agreements about queuing, truth-telling, not humiliating people simply because you can - were never glamorous, but for a while they held.

That is what has started to fray. Earlier generations were drilled, often harshly, in a simple creed: you are part of something bigger, and when it matters, you sacrifice for it. As that story has faded, it hasn't been replaced by a new, coherent common good. It has been replaced by a marketplace of identities and causes, each demanding loyalty on its own terms.

Without some agreed centre of gravity, the gaps widen. People retreat from the messy, frustrating middle into tribes that promise clarity and moral certainty. It stops being about what we owe a country, a neighbourhood or a broad 'us' and becomes about defending the honour of people exactly like you. The more politics turns into a clash of wounded mirrors, the easier it is to justify extremes.

You can see that in the rise of groups who proudly organise around confrontation. At the radical edges of the left, antifa activists frame themselves as militant anti-fascists, willing to use doxing, harassment, property damage and street fights to 'deplatform' their enemies. On the far right, outfits like the Proud Boys in North America or the National Socialist Network in Australia wrap misogyny, radical racism and white-nationalist fantasies in the language of 'Western chauvinism', 'free speech' or 'white pride', and turn up at rallies dressed for a brawl.

The slogans are different to the twentieth-century cunts, but the underlying music is the same. We are righteous, they are vermin, and violence is an acceptable way to express that. The moustaches are worse; the impulse is familiar.

CRACKS IN WHO WE THINK WE ARE

Underneath all the shouting, there's a quieter crisis; we no longer agree on what it means to be a decent human. For a long time, most people in the West at least mouthed the same basics: you grow up, you take on responsibility, you try to tell the truth, you keep your promises, you don't leave the weak to drown. The scripts were flawed and often unfair, especially around gender and race, but there were scripts. Now those old scripts are collapsing faster than new ones can bed in.

THE MANOSPHERE

Traditional masculinity – provider, protector, emotionally closed – has been challenged, but nothing solid has replaced it, so a lot of young men feel accused, surplus or directionless and go looking for certainty in all the wrong places. Instead of adult responsibility, some slink off into sulking, porn, streaming and gaming platforms, conspiracy podcasts and online gurus in sunglasses explaining that real men drive supercars and women are basically walking problems to be managed.

A myriad of women hating misogynists have basically turned radicalisation into a multi-level marketing scheme: sign up today for your complimentary starter kit of grievance, misogyny and mirror selfies – no actual achievements required. The whole thing is like cosplay adulthood, boys rehearsing being 'dangerous' men by quoting podcasts at each other in Discord chats their mums are still paying the Wi-Fi for.

You've now got teenage guys mainlining clips about 'alphas', 'high-value men' and 'female nature' like it's self-help, when really it's just an emotional support group for avoiding basic responsibility, emotional literacy and laundry. They're furious at women, immigrants, 'elites' and anyone else within blaming distance, essentially everyone except the person in the bathroom mirror with the ring light.

And into that stew, someone's decided it's a good idea to start feeding translated Hitler speeches like they're just another 'motivational' sound for gym edits. You scroll from a guy explaining why women shouldn't vote to a colour-graded clip of a genocidal dictator being treated like a misunderstood life coach, as if the real lesson of the twentieth century was 'speak with confidence and don't skip leg day'.

THE FOURTH WAVE

On the other side of the screen, young women are being hypersexualised from puberty onwards, marinated in Instagram bodies, porn-adjacent 'wellness' content and hookup-culture PR, with influencers turning 'hot mess but flawless' into a full-time aesthetic. The internet sells it all as a vibe. You're not being objectified; you're just 'in your glow-up era', conveniently branded, filtered and available on demand. The pipeline runs from VSCO girl to soft-launching a situationship to an experimental OnlyFans trial period, and the invoice doesn't arrive until years later, when the views have dropped but the screenshots haven't.

By then, the fine print is brutal. Former porn stars turned wives and mothers sit in podcasts and interviews, asking the world to forget what the internet is specifically designed never to forget, begging for scenes to be scrubbed so their kids won't stumble across them, so strangers will finally stop recognising them at the supermarket or school gates. They talk about being young, broke, love-bombed by 'agents' and boyfriends, convinced they were taking control of their sexuality, only to realise they'd just given permanent licensing rights to their most intimate moments. It's hard to 'rebrand' when the algorithm keeps dragging your past out of the archives for anyone who types your name slightly wrong.

Meanwhile, today's girls are told they must be endlessly capable, independent, nurturing, sexually liberated and always 'up for it', as if feminism were a productivity hack rather than a political project. They are expected to be mental-load managers, emotional support units, top-tier professionals and amateur porn performers all in one, and many feel pressured into doing things they don't actually want to do because saying no risks being labelled frigid, boring or instantly replaceable by the next For You Page clone. Consent becomes less about what they want and more about what will keep the vibe going, the group chat approving and the situationship intact.

One minute the script says 'smash the patriarchy and never need a man', the next it says 'be a perfect partner and mother and also have a killer career and also look 27 forever and also treat sex like a brand collaboration'. It's feminism as a constantly updating operating system, with endless patch notes but the same old bugs. Men still paid more, women still blamed more, platforms still profited more. The message is: you can be anything you want, as long as you are also hot, chill, sexually adventurous, financially independent, emotionally low-maintenance and willing to turn your most private experiences into content.

THE RESULTING CHAOS

So boys get sold a fantasy of power without responsibility, and girls get sold a fantasy of empowerment that still mostly serves other people's desires. Both sides of the screen are being scripted by the same machine, one that doesn't care who gets hurt as long as engagement stays high. And in the middle are actual teenagers, trying to figure out love, sex and identity while being coached by a chorus of influencers, ex-influencers and regretful veterans of the content economy who keep proving, in real time, that the internet remembers everything except the context.

Nobody can meet those demands without breaking somewhere. When you are being measured against impossible checklists, algorithms and influencers from every direction, resentment, self-absorption and retreating into cartoon versions of masculinity and femininity start to feel like reasonable coping strategies.

THE FLUID NATURE OF BIOLOGY

Layered over the top of this is a furious argument about sex and gender itself. For most of human history, most people were handed a very simple script at birth. You're a boy or you're a girl; here is what that means, and get on with it. Those scripts were often suffocating and cruel, especially for anyone who didn't fit the mould, and a lot of what we call 'gender progress' is just people refusing to keep pretending those boxes worked for everyone.

At the same time, we've lurched from rigid certainty to something close to free-for-all. In the space of a decade, ideas that were once niche have gone mainstream: that gender is a spectrum, that it can be 'fluid', that how you feel inside outranks what your body is made of. Adults can barely keep up with the new language. Kids are being asked, in some schools and online spaces, to declare identities they barely understand before they've worked out how to ride a bike.

The basic biological reality – that humans come in male and female bodies, with a minority who experience that as a source of deep distress – has not disappeared. What has changed is the story we tell about what follows from that. Instead of starting from 'your body is real, and we'll help you live well in it, whatever your personality looks like', we have drifted towards 'if your personality doesn't match the stereotype, maybe your body is the problem'.

THINK OF THE CHILDREN

For vulnerable kids, especially those who are lonely, autistic, same-sex attracted, traumatised or just uncomfortable in their skin, otherwise known as 'teenagers', this can be a minefield. One side treats any questioning of gender norms as dangerous nonsense and any distressed child as a would-be activist. The other treats discomfort with your body as proof you were 'born in the wrong one', and scepticism as bigotry. Somewhere in the middle are actual children, trying to form an identity while the adults throw acronyms at each other.

This isn't about hating trans or non-binary people. There are adults who have lived with gender dysphoria for years, thought hard, made difficult choices and just want to be left alone to get on with life. They are not the problem. The problem is a culture that has turned a serious, complex condition into a fashion, a political football and, for some, a catch-all explanation for every kind of teenage pain.

When you tell an entire generation that both biology and gender are infinitely negotiable, but also that getting it wrong makes you a bad person, you shouldn't be surprised when confusion, anxiety and anger go through the roof. As with so many things in the Age of Me, the extremism on both sides feeds into societal cunthood. One side uses the existence of a tiny minority to demand total obedience to ever-shifting language rules; the other uses that overreach to justify cruelty and blanket contempt, and the kids who mainly needed time, patience and boundaries are left to clean up the mess.

THE RISE OF THE TRIBE

In that confusion, it becomes easier to retreat into smaller, simpler identities, your fandom, your politics, your grievance group, your online tribe. Instead of seeing yourself as a flawed citizen among other flawed citizens, you appoint yourself the representative of 'real men', 'real women', 'the oppressed', 'the forgotten', and everyone outside your circle becomes an abstraction or a threat. Basic humanity starts to thin out. People aren't people anymore; they're symbols in your argument.

You can hear the shift in the way we talk. The old questions, 'What kind of person do I want to be? What kind of life do I want to build?', are being crowded out by 'How do I show up? How do I feel about myself? Do I feel seen?' When appearance and self-esteem become more important than character, cunthood stops being something you slide into reluctantly on a bad day and becomes a position you can defend. 'I did what I had to do for me' becomes the trump card that ends the conversation.

REWRITING THE STORY AS WE GO

There's another undercurrent to all this – the way we keep rewriting the script of who we are to please whoever's shouting the loudest. Every generation picks a fight with its own history, but right now we're in a full-blown renovation phase. Whole eras are getting scrubbed, polished or turned into political ammunition depending on which tribe you're in and what today's outrage menu happens to be: colonialism, gender, race, crime, genocide, take your pick.

Of course, there's nothing new about redrafting the past. The Ancient Egyptians were masters of the delete key long before social media made it fashionable. When a pharaoh fell out of favour, their name was chiselled off temples and obelisks as if they'd never existed. Akhenaten and his queen Nefertiti tried to start fresh with a sun-god cult and a new capital at Amarna, but after their deaths, their successors put a swift end to that experiment – city dismantled, religion cancelled, names erased. It's one of history's earliest examples of revisionism, proof that even the ancients loved a good narrative reboot.

On one side, you get a glossy rerun of the 'good old days', all discipline, respect and neatly pressed morals, with the racism, domestic violence and casual cruelty quietly cropped out of frame. Colonisation gets rebranded as 'nation-building', empire recast as a noble 'civilising mission', and anyone who dares to mention the invoice paid by Indigenous peoples or colonised nations is swiftly accused of disloyalty, as if acknowledging harm were the same thing as hating home.

On the other side, you get a sweeping narrative in which everything that came before us was nothing but oppression, so the only morally acceptable posture is to sneer at your grandparents, pull down their statues and declare the whole project irredeemable. Both moves are dishonest in different ways, and both conveniently let us avoid the harder question. What have we actually built with the freedom and prosperity we inherited? In political rhetoric, whole parties are recast as fascists or communists depending on your feed, while words like 'terrorist', 'Nazi' and 'groomer' get flung around so casually they may as well be punctuation. A death on one side is framed as an unforgivable act of terrorism, while a death on the other is 'regrettable but necessary' or 'legitimate self-defence'.

The killing of thousands in one direction is denounced as genocide by a colonising power, while many of the same voices fall curiously silent when thousands die trying to overthrow a violent, religiously extreme regime that has been brutalising its own people for years. The content changes – colonialism, gender ideology, migration, crime, genocide – but the technique is the same. Flatten the past and present into a morality play where you and your side are always on the right page of history, and the worth of a human life quietly rises or falls depending on the flag over the coffin.

REVISIONISM 101

This kind of revisionism dissolves any stable sense of 'we'. If your history lessons and media bubble tell you your country has always been basically heroic, then anyone who criticises it looks like a traitor. If they tell you it has always been basically wicked, then anyone who feels any attachment to it looks like a fool or an accomplice. In both cases, there's no room left for ordinary, complicated love of place and people, the kind of love that can admit horror and still say, 'This is ours; we need to make it better.'

When you can't tell a shared story about where you came from, it's much harder to agree on where you're going, or why you should sacrifice anything for people you'll never meet. And whenever the story lurches too far in one direction, a counter-story rushes in. The louder some voices declare the past shameful and the present infinitely malleable, the more room they create for demagogues who promise to restore 'how things were'.

That's how you end up with strongmen and would-be strongmen railing against 'wokeness', 'globalism' and 'gender ideology', offering a return to order, tradition and 'common sense' to people who feel disoriented and mocked by rapid change. They talk about protecting 'our way of life' while quietly recycling the same scapegoats and resentments that powered the historical cunts of the twentieth century. The names change, the speeches get better lighting, but the basic move is the same: it was better before, and it's their fault.

And the swing works the other way too. The more loudly some voices insist that everything was fine before, that the past was orderly, that men were men, women were women, the borders were secure and nobody complained, the more room they create for a different kind of fanatic who wants to dissolve any limit at all.

That's how you end up with activists and would-be moral entrepreneurs insisting that every boundary is violence, every tradition is oppression and every hesitation is hate, offering a vision of the world where feelings are law and reality is whatever your group says it is. They talk about liberation and inclusion while quietly demanding total obedience to ever-shifting language codes and purity tests. The slogans change, the haircuts get more interesting, but the basic move is the same: it will be perfect soon, and if it isn't, it's because of them.

Underneath all the slogans and culture-war skirmishes, that's what revisionism at both extremes achieves. It saws through the last, creaking beams of common identity. Once those go, all that's left is you and your chosen micro-tribes, glaring at everyone else across an ever-widening gap. That's the perfect breeding ground for cunthood, because there's no longer any solid 'us' to betray, only 'them' to attack and 'me' to defend.

THE QUIET COLLAPSE OF TRUST AND CIVILITY

When you hollow out shared stories of who we are and what we owe each other, trust starts to leak away. You can see it in data if you like charts, but you don't need them. You can feel it.

Neighbours are less likely to know each other. Institutions are more likely to be treated as scams until proven otherwise. Every scandal confirms the suspicion that the game is rigged. 'Most people can be trusted' has quietly turned into 'assume the worst and you won't be disappointed'. Civility goes with it. If you spend enough time in online spaces where the default tone is sneering, abusive or panicked, it changes how you think real people think. You start from bad faith.

A clumsy sentence is treated as deliberate malice. A disagreement is 'violence'. In that state, quoting strangers out of context for sport becomes normal, attributing the worst possible motives to the other side becomes instinct, and public humiliation becomes a first response rather than a last resort.

Your relationship with reality itself gets bent. When every feed is an angry collage of genuine news, half-truths, clipped outrage and outright lies, and the stuff that upsets you is what gets pushed to the top, the temptation is simple: if it flatters my side, it must be true; if it offends me, it must be false. Facts become optional. What matters is whether a story keeps your identity intact.

The result is a society where people increasingly occupy different worlds while technically sharing the same streets. They're watching different versions of events, using different vocabularies for the same things and accusing each other of living in 'fantasy land'. If you've ever tried to talk to a relative at a family barbeque, who has gone deep into a particular media or conspiracy rabbit hole, you know the feeling. You're not arguing over opinions. You're arguing over the facts that exist in their head.

4

CUNTS IN THE WILD

FIELD TRAINING — COASTAL TOWN RACISM

As one of the only kids of Lebanese descent, growing up in a small coastal town in Australia in the 1980s, it was not the sun-bleached, everyone-mates-with-everyone postcard it likes to remember itself as. The White Australia Policy had only officially been buried about a decade earlier, and you could still feel the hangover in the air, in classrooms, on footy fields, behind shop counters. The marketing material said 'multicultural', but the operating system still said 'don't get too dark'.

Plenty of people were kind, or at least too busy surviving to care what colour your dad was. But there were plenty of ill-informed cunts who used racism like punctuation, something to reach for whenever they wanted to feel a bit bigger. Kids parrot what they hear at home, so the taunts came early and fluently. 'Wog', 'Lebanese prick', 'garlic breath', 'go back to where you came from' – all the classics, delivered by children who didn't wake up thinking, 'How can I be a racist little prick today?' They were marinating in what their parents and grandparents, the remnants of the so-called Silent Generation, fed them as normal.

That generation gave us a lot of hard work and stoicism, yes, but also a fair bit of bottled-up rage, ignorance and the kind of casual racism that could strip the paint off a fence post. Teachers mispronouncing your name for the fifth year running and acting like it was adorable. Shopkeepers watching you just a little too closely. Parents at sporting events making comments just loud enough for you to hear, but just quiet enough that you couldn't easily call them on it.

So I learned quickly where I sat in the local pecking order: brownish, foreign-ish, good at sport if I wanted some protection and always slightly on trial. My worth, in a lot of eyes, was negotiable. It could be knocked down a few notches with a joke, a slur, a lazy assumption.

This is not my retiring Australian cricketer of South Asian descent moment. I'm not standing on some metaphorical cricket pavilion making a grand retirement statement about racism before walking off into the sunset, having represented my country at the highest level and with a multimillion-dollar property portfolio to cushion the landing. I'm still very much in the cheap seats, trying to explain that the pitch was never level to begin with, while being politely advised to just be grateful I got a game at all.

Most of these people would have been outraged to be called racist. They were 'just having a laugh', 'just saying what everyone's thinking', 'just telling it like it is'. The usual disclaimers cunts use when they haven't yet graduated to a mirror. That was the atmosphere, low-level, constant, corrosive. But my first proper interaction with a full-time, professional-grade cunt wasn't a kid in the playground or some old bloke at the RSL muttering about 'bloody wogs'. It was Bruno over the back fence.

BRUNO – THE ORIGINAL FIELD SPECIMEN

In 1980, my parents moved us to a new estate on the mid-north coast of New South Wales. 'Estate' is generous. At that stage, it was mostly banana plantations, dreams and a display home. My father bought a block and decided he'd build the house himself because he was Lebanese, it was the eighties and Bunnings hadn't yet broken the spirit of the DIY man. There was just one existing house in the street. It belonged to Bruno and his wife, Roberta.

Bruno was an Italian migrant from Sicily with halting English, a thick accent and that warm, slightly chaotic energy a lot of migrant dads had back then. Initially, he and my father bonded over the international language of concrete, cigarettes and complaining about councils. Roberta and my mother did the driveway diplomacy: bags of tomatoes over the fence, 'Merry Christmas' shouted from one yard to the other, quick coffee chats about kids and bills and weather.

To a kid like me, who was already used to being reminded I was different by the broader town, this little pocket of migrant solidarity meant something. The grown-ups slipped between languages. There were smells from kitchens that didn't come out of *The Australian Women's Weekly*. The message was simple: out there, you're the outsider; in here, you're one of us.

Bruno had a Harley, which, when you're a small boy in a sandy new estate, might as well be a spaceship. This was not some sensible commuter bike. In my memory, it's huge, loud, full of chrome and fumes and danger. He would take us kids for rides up and down the street, one at a time, helmet too big, arms wrapped around this leather-clad adult god as the engine shook under us.

Those rides were magic. The whole street would tilt. For thirty seconds at a time, we weren't the weird family with the foreign dad and the funny food; we were flying. The roar of the Harley drowned out everything: the neighbours, the schoolyard, the kids who couldn't quite say your name right but could nail the insults. Bruno, in those moments, was the cool neighbour with the bike, not a case study.

And that's important. Cunts rarely walk into your life wearing a name tag. They arrive as charm, as favours, as rides on the Harley. They show you the fun side first. They make sure there's something you'll miss when they turn.

Because Bruno did turn.

At first it was small stuff. The warmth cooled. The Harley rides stopped. The wave across the street turned into a nod, then a grunt, then just a stare. Complaints began about bins, about whose leaves were blowing where, about parking. Typical neighbour static, the sort of thing you could file under 'old blokes are like that' if you squinted.

Then the truth came through the plasterboard. Bruno was beating Roberta. If you've never had domestic violence break through the suburban wallpaper, it is hard to explain how obscene it feels. This is the same house you've seen Christmas decorations on. The same people you've clinked glasses with in the street. And suddenly Roberta is at our front door in tears, bruises on her arms and face, asking if she can come in for a while because 'he's angry again'.

My mother would sit her at the kitchen table, clean her up, make coffee, because in migrant households, coffee is the first line of defence against literally everything, and quietly suggest doctors, police, services. The things you say when you're trying to get someone out of hell without making them feel any more ashamed.

One day, Roberta begged my father to drive her to the local RSL. She was convinced Bruno was there with his mistress and wanted to catch him in the act. My father listened, looked at her, and said he'd gladly drive her to the hospital or the police station, but he wasn't going to drive her to a stakeout so she could watch more of her life implode. Even for him, there were limits to the services offered by a friendly neighbour.

Eventually, mercifully, Roberta left. She moved to Sydney to live with her son. Bruno stayed. He had his house, his freedom and, as far as anyone could tell, his mistress. You might hope that would be the end of it. The cunt loses his punching bag and is forced to sit alone with himself and a slowly overcooked cotoletta.

Bruno had other plans.

At the time, my mother had a cleaner who came to the house a couple of times a week. A hard-working woman. Got in, did the job, went home. At some point, Bruno decided she was his next opportunity. When she didn't respond the way he wanted, which I'm going to guess was anything from 'good morning' to 'I will leave my family for you, Bruno, you irresistible god', he marched over to our place, knocked on the door and told my mother she needed to fire, in his words, 'the whore'.

My mother, who had a very particular look reserved for men talking out of their arse, let him finish and then explained, calmly, that who she employed was none of his business, what the woman did outside work was none of her business, and if he insisted on using language like that again he could go and discuss it with someone who gave a shit. This was not verbatim, but close enough.

That was the day Bruno declared war on our family.

From then on, it was a one-man campaign of petty spite. Rubbish from his yard mysteriously migrated onto our verge. Fires mysteriously flared up along the fence line on the precise days my mother was washing every sheet in the house. Random complaints started appearing at the council. You could feel his eyes on you in a way that says, 'Everything you do I will treat as an attack.'

For me, who'd already spent years swallowing little racist digs from schoolmates who 'didn't mean anything by it', Bruno was like a masterclass in cunthood. The town's background racism chipped away at my understanding of my self-worth, and Bruno demonstrated to me what happens when someone builds their entire identity on the same basic logic. I matter, you don't, and if you forget that for a second, I'll remind you.

After weeks of trying to keep things civil and talk it through like grown-ups, my father finally snapped. One afternoon, it boiled over into a full-blown shouting match across the back fence, Bruno in one yard, my old man in the other, both of them windmilling their arms and slipping between English and their mother tongues like a pair of furious UN interpreters on too much espresso.

At one point, Dad was so furious he slipped into abusing Bruno in Arabic, to which Mum, ever the linguist, calmly observed, 'He can't understand you when you speak in Arabic.' Without breaking stride, Dad switched back into his best broken English so he could resume threatening him in a language Bruno did understand. Think less UN Security Council and more an SBS-subtitled episode of *Neighbours* directed by Martin Scorsese. From our slightly elevated block, I could see half the suburb out on their balconies and verandas, craning their necks to work out what these two wogs were screaming at each other in mangled English, like they were getting live theatre with their afternoon tea.

You'd like to think the police came in as neutral adults and calmed things down. What actually happened is my father went to the local police station, explained the situation, and the superintendent, who knew my father well, said something along the lines of 'Look, officially, there's not much we can do ... Unofficially? Just punch him in the face.' That was community policing in the golden era, a laminated charter on the wall and 'just king-hit him' over the counter.

Meanwhile, while I was away at boarding school – supposedly studying but actually discovering girls and terrible beer – my local mates decided to enlist themselves in the backyard war. Unbeknownst to me, they started running midnight missions: stealing Bruno's letterbox, urinating in his water tank, all the usual strokes of teenage genius. When I came home for the Christmas break, Bruno accused me of nicking his letterbox three times. I tried to explain that I'd been away at boarding school for the entire school term, but he wasn't buying it. The next day, I dropped by my mate Tim's place and spotted three number six letterboxes stacked against the fence. They thought they were helping. In reality, they'd just written themselves into the same soap opera.

The same man who once let us kids cling to his leather jacket on Harley rides up and down the street had become, by any reasonable measure, a full-time, professional cunt. Violent at home, vindictive in the street, permanently cast as the hero in his own internal drama. And that's the shape I've recognised ever since, in far fancier packaging. Once you've met one Bruno, and once you've grown up breathing in the low-level cunthood of casual racism, you start seeing the pattern everywhere.

They don't all hit. They don't all live in fibro houses. Some of them wear spandex and frequent your favourite coffee shop. Some of them don suits and move in elite business and political circles. Some of them have Instagram accounts and ring lights. What they share is the basic Bruno template: my wants first, my pride sacred, my grievance holy, everyone else collateral.

Let's go find them.

HOW WE CONSUME – THE CUSTOMER IS ALWAYS RIGHT BRUNO

When I was growing up, you went to the shop, bought something and hoped it worked. If it didn't, you took it back, muttered 'bloody useless' and maybe quietly tried a different shop next time. There was a sort of social truce. Sellers tried not to rip you off. Buyers tried not to be pricks. When it went wrong, nobody assumed it was a personal attack from the universe.

Somewhere along the way that truce got rewritten into a slogan: the customer is always right. What the original saying actually meant was much narrower – the customer is always right in matters of taste. If someone wants a purple hat with feathers, you sell them the purple hat. You don't argue about their preferences. But somewhere between department stores and drive-through coffee, the second half of that sentence quietly disappeared. The idea mutated into a kind of retail theology in which the person holding the receipt is automatically correct about everything, and the nineteen-year-old behind the counter is personally responsible for fixing the emotional state of the entire interaction.

Fast-forward to today. We've spent the last few decades telling people they are not customers; they are 'guests', 'members', 'VIPs'. The coffee chain calls you 'family'. The telco sends you a text about how 'we're in this together'. Everything from an app to a supermarket loyalty card is sold as a personalised experience. The Age of Me has turned buying a coffee into a referendum on your self-worth. It was one of those small, almost forgettable moments that only reveal their significance in hindsight.

The café was busy, the usual morning rhythm unfolding around us. Orders were called, cups clattered, conversations blurred into background noise. And then the coffee arrived, made with the wrong brand of oat milk. I have watched people lose their minds over this. Grown adults. Suits. Parents. People with mortgages. A barista, who is barely nineteen and has been awake since 5 am, puts the wrong milk in a coffee and suddenly they are Hitler.

There's a raised voice, a tapping finger, the phrase 'unacceptable' thrown around as if we're in a royal commission. You see the move, straight from 'slightly annoyed' to 'I'd like to speak to your manager' to 'I will be making a formal complaint' to 'I have five thousand followers and I'll be posting about this'. Basic mistakes transformed into moral crimes, with a side order of public shaming.

In a disturbingly advanced edition of the same performance, a man in a sandwich shop in Atlanta, Georgia, decided that 'too much mayonnaise' wasn't a minor hiccup but a line in the sand. He treated a rookie worker like a war criminal, stormed out, came back with a gun, and turned a condiment quibble into a crime scene by murdering the two employees.

Bruno with a loyalty card one coffee away from a freebie.

HOW WE DATE – BRUNO SWIPING RIGHT

Romance brings out a different subspecies of Bruno, the one who can look you in the eye over tapas and say, 'I'm just really big on honesty,' and somehow forget to mention the long-term partner, the joint mortgage and the Tinder profile that's been 'accidentally' active since 2016. In this ecosystem, 'not looking for anything serious' means 'I absolutely am, just not with you', 'taking it slow' means 'keeping my options open', and 'bad at texting' means 'very good at texting, just not your number'.

First dates are full of stories about toxic exes, crazy exes and manipulative exes. The only common factor, strangely, is the person telling the story. Most of the time, the damage is small and deniable. Someone ghosts after three nice dates. Someone breadcrumbs you with just enough attention to keep you circling while they 'figure themselves out' on three other dating apps. Someone gives you the full couple experience, shared playlists, a toothbrush at their place, 'meet my friends', then suddenly remembers they're 'not in the right headspace' the moment you ask what this actually is.

Everyone kind of knows the game and pretends they don't, because being single is already a horror show and you just want to believe that this time, maybe, the love-bombing means love, not unexploded ordnance.

If the first-date charmer is Bruno at the open home, the long-term situationship is Bruno on a month-to-month lease. The good ones are up-front. 'I like you, I'm not available, here are my limits.' The Bruno type discovers they can rule the emotional schedule from behind a string of half-apologies and 'busy weeks'. They never quite say you're their partner, but they never quite let you go. They talk about 'seeing where it goes' whenever you ask for clarity, disappear the moment you need support, and then reappear when you try to move on, suddenly full of insight about how 'special' your connection is.

On an average day, this looks like plans that are always 'last minute', birthdays 'forgotten' while their crises are treated as national emergencies, you learning to read three dots on a screen like tea leaves. Friends gently ask what you're getting out of it. You answer with things Bruno once said at 1:17 am on a Tuesday, when they were lonely and mildly drunk. People grumble in group chats, but the arrangement rolls on because nobody wants to be the one who turns 'it's complicated' into 'it's over'.

In a deluxe version of how we date, Bruno really goes to work. One man on Tinder decided that being a moderately charming human with a decent haircut wasn't nearly ambitious enough, so he upgraded himself to the son of a billionaire diamond tycoon under constant threat from shadowy enemies. Private jets, luxury hotels, designer clothes – the full cinematic experience. Women weren't just meeting a man; they were stepping into a plot. The romance moved fast, the gestures were extravagant, and before long the dramatic twist arrived: enemies were after him, his accounts were frozen, his security team was in danger, and tragically the only thing standing between him and catastrophe was a girlfriend with a healthy credit limit.

And so the money flowed. Loans, credit cards, transfers, all sent to keep their endangered billionaire safe. The clever part was that the money wasn't protecting him from enemies at all; it was funding the next girlfriend's private jet date. A romantic Ponzi scheme powered by charm, urgency and the phrase 'my enemies are after me.' Eventually the curtain lifted and the diamond heir turned out to be a man whose real empire was audacity – The Tinder Swindler.

Bruno, just with better lighting, a private jet, and someone else's credit limit.

HOW WE PARENT – BRUNO JUNIOR

Once upon a time, if a kid fell off their bike the standard parenting protocol was fairly simple: you alright? If the answer was yes, you got back on the bike. If the answer was no, someone's mum appeared with a Band-Aid and possibly a biscuit, and life continued. Childhood was a slightly chaotic apprenticeship in gravity, disappointment and the occasional scraped knee.

Then along came Parenting Bruno, and suddenly the child is no longer a small human learning how the world works. The child is a project, a brand, and occasionally a fragile diplomatic mission that must be shielded from all possible adversity. This is the helicopter edition of

Bruno – permanently hovering, scanning the horizon for threats like a suburban air-defence system.

You see it first at school. The teacher suggests little Oliver might need to work harder at maths and Bruno doesn't hear feedback, he hears an attack on the family empire. Emails are written. Meetings are requested. The possibility that Oliver simply didn't study is dismissed immediately. Much more plausible is a conspiracy involving poor teaching, inadequate curriculum design and the broader collapse of Western civilisation.

The deluxe edition appeared in Sydney, when a father from an elite private school threatened legal action after his son was suspended from the school rugby team following disciplinary issues. What should have been a routine life lesson, break the rules, miss the game, instead escalated into lawyers, formal complaints and arguments about the boy's future sporting prospects. A school discipline matter was upgraded, with impressive speed, into something approaching a commercial dispute.

Bruno with a stroller and a firm belief that little Oliver should probably be the CEO his first day on the job.

HOW WE WORK – CORPORATE BRUNO

Then there's work. Offices. Teams. Organisations. All those places where adults go to wear their 'professional' mask and then do exactly the same petty shit they did in the playground, just with better stationery.

On paper, modern workplaces are temples of virtue. Every organisation has a vision statement. A values page. Posters about respect and inclusion in the kitchen, printed in at least three calming colours. Managers talk about 'psychological safety' and 'bringing your whole self to work', which is ironic because the whole self they usually want is the bit that meets KPIs and doesn't complain.

Underneath the posters, the old habits are still there. The boss who publicly denounces bullying while privately protecting the office bully because 'they get results'. The colleague who never raises an issue to your face but loves writing a 'just looping in everyone' email that makes you look like an idiot in front of twenty people. The manager who gives a heartfelt speech about wellbeing and then drops three people's jobs on one person and calls it 'a growth opportunity'.

At the lanyard-heavy end of town, it just gets more expensive. One senior executive did exactly what the poster in the kitchen tells you to do: she lodged a formal complaint about being bullied by a director. Boxes ticked, values 'lived'. The response wasn't to fix the behaviour. Oh no, it was to quietly ice *her* out, responsibilities stripped, key meetings 'forgotten', a gentle consensus forming that she was 'the issue', until she was shown the door under the banner of 'performance' and 'restructure'. A court later called it what it was and handed over a few million reasons not to confuse 'process' with justice.

Bruno with a human resources policy.

HOW WE DRIVE — ROAD RAGE BRUNO

If you ever want to know who someone really is, sit in the passenger seat while they drive. Don't ask them about their values. Don't ask them how they see themselves. Just watch what happens when someone pulls in front of them without indicating. Driving is one of the last places where most adults are unsupervised. No boss. No partner. No HR. No Instagram Live (yet). Just you, a car and a bunch of strangers also trying to get somewhere. It is a perfect little lab for how you handle frustration when nobody you care about is watching.

You know the type. You might be the type on a bad day. The person who cannot stand to let one car merge in front of him and will actually speed up to close the gap, even though the entire traffic jam is going to be sitting at the same red light thirty seconds later. The person who tailgates so close she may as well be in your boot because you had the audacity to stick to the school zone limit. The person who lays on the horn the instant a light turns green, as if their Toyota Corolla has somewhere extremely important to be.

Every now and then you get the deluxe edition. In Western Sydney, one bloke decided that letting another driver merge around a parked car at a roundabout was a bridge too far. He cut him off to block the gap, they both stopped, there were words, and then he took off with the other man pinned to the side of his ute, dragging him along the road until he went under the rear wheel and died. Over a few metres of lane and a dented ego, he traded his licence for a manslaughter conviction and sixteen years to think about merging.

Bruno with a driver's licence.

HOW WE TRADE — ESTATE AGENT BRUNO

Real estate brings out a very particular subspecies of Bruno: the person who can look you in the eye, tell you a story that is technically adjacent to the truth, and sleep like a baby on a mattress stuffed with disclaimers. They call a one-bedroom flat with a hotplate a 'chef's kitchen', traffic noise 'urban energy', and a mould problem 'ripe for your personal touch'. They 'forget' to mention the development application next door, the pending six-figure special levy, or the fact that the lovely 'long-term tenants' haven't paid rent since the last Olympics.

Most of the time the damage is slow and spread out. A buyer overpays. A seller is flattered into under-listing. A renter signs a lease for a place that smells like wet carpet and regret once the scented candle has been removed. Everyone sort of knows the game and pretends they don't, because housing is already stressful enough and at some point you just want the keys to your slice of the Australian dream.

The deluxe edition appeared recently in Sydney when a real estate agent was stripped of their licence by regulators for systematic underquoting. Properties were advertised tens or hundreds of thousands below where the agent knew the reserve actually sat. First-home buyers turned up to inspections thinking they had a shot. By auction day the price floated magically far above the 'guide', leaving bidders bewildered and the agent with a crowded auction and a healthier commission. Inside their own head, this is just marketing. From the outside it looks more like selling hope at a discount and reality at a premium.

Bruno with a listing agreement.

HOW WE GOVERN – STRATA MANAGER BRUNO

If the real estate agent is Bruno at the point of sale, the strata manager is Bruno on retainer. The good ones quietly keep the place upright. They organise insurance, chase repairs and translate the strange language of by-laws into something resembling common sense. Buildings run smoothly and nobody notices them, which is exactly how the job is supposed to work.

Strata Manager Bruno discovers something different: you can run an entire building from behind a keyboard and an invoice. Emails they don't like mysteriously go unanswered. By-laws are quoted like scripture when it suits them and quietly forgotten when it doesn't. Contractors appear who are oddly familiar with the manager and slightly less familiar with competitive pricing. Every invoice contains a small 'admin fee' that nobody quite remembers approving. On an average day this looks like repairs that take eighteen months, pets being rejected in buildings that voted for pets three AGMs ago, and a manager who treats owners like naughty children interrupting something important.

The deluxe edition appeared on the Mid North Coast of New South Wales, where a strata manager was banned and prosecuted after siphoning millions of dollars from trust accounts belonging to the very buildings she managed. Owners paid their levies assuming the money was sitting safely in regulated accounts for insurance, maintenance and repairs. Instead large portions quietly migrated into the manager's personal accounts until the hole became impossible to hide.

By the time regulators stepped in, the schemes involved were staring at empty trust balances and years of financial damage – proof that when Strata Manager Bruno really commits to the role, the sinking fund doesn't just shrink. It disappears.

Bruno with the trust account banking login.

HOW WE LIVE — COMMON PROPERTY BRUNO

Neighbourhoods used to be simple. You moved in, you said hello to your neighbour and you tried not to be a dick. If you were, someone's dad sorted it out over the fence and everyone had a beer afterwards. Then strata arrived. The simple idea of 'live near each other' acquired a legal framework, shared drains and a compulsory AGM. A lot of good comes with that. Shared buildings need rules. Roofs need fixing, lifts need maintaining, pipes need replacing and money needs to be collected from people who would rather spend it elsewhere.

But strata also provides fertile soil for Brunos. On paper an owners corporation is a group of adults managing a shared asset. In practice it is often a handful of people who have discovered they can turn minor preferences into crusades. Meetings fill with arguments about whether anything should be done about the committee chair illegally occupying a room on common property because, as someone eventually points out, 'it doesn't affect my lot'. When the legal risk is explained – that if another owner later discovers the unlawful use and the owners corporation knowingly ignored it, the entire scheme could be dragged into legal action – heads nod thoughtfully. Then someone inevitably asks, 'Yes, but who would actually do that?' It is the administrative equivalent of refusing to put fuel in the car because it is still rolling downhill.

Then come the tree wars. One owner wants shade, another wants views, and instead of talking like adults – 'how about we prune it every year?' – the dispute escalates immediately to poisoning roots, council complaints, arborist reports and lawyers copied into email chains. Entire weekends, friendships and committee meetings evaporate because nobody can tolerate the possibility that they might not get exactly what they want on land they only partly own.

The deluxe edition arrived in a Sydney apartment building where a dispute began because one resident pressed the lift button before others finished loading furniture. A tiny irritation, the kind normal adults forget about within minutes. Common Property Bruno saw something else entirely. Months of complaints followed. Emails multiplied. Notices appeared. Eventually one resident began jamming the lift doors and disabling the mechanism, apparently to teach everyone else respect. The owners corporation spent tens of thousands of dollars repairing the damage while investigators tried to understand why the building's lift had become the site of psychological warfare.

Inside Bruno's head he was defending standards. From the outside it was a man vandalising common property because someone pressed a button too early. A minor inconvenience promoted into a moral crusade.

Bruno with a proxy form.

HOW WE REVIEW — ONE STAR BRUNO

Once upon a time, if you didn't like a place, you just didn't go back. Maybe you muttered to a friend, 'Bit shit, that one,' and that was the end of it. Now, every transaction comes with homework. 'Please rate your experience.' 'How did we do today?' 'Tell us what you think!' The Age of Me heard that and said, 'Gladly.' Most people use reviews the way they're supposed to: a quick note that the food was good but the music was loud, or the delivery arrived on time but the box looked like it had lost a fight with a forklift.

Then there's Star-Rating Bruno. The person who treats the review screen like a loaded weapon, aimed squarely at whoever annoyed them that day. They leave one-star epics because their Uber driver wouldn't break the road rules, or because a café refused to honour a discount that expired in 2019, or because a receptionist asked them to wait their turn. The text is less 'here's what happened' and more 'here is my 1,200-word character assessment of a stranger who did not instantly intuit my needs'.

In a disturbingly deluxe edition of the same performance, One-Star Bruno doesn't just leave a review, he mobilises a militia. In 2022, a small café in Australia refused service to a customer who arrived after closing. The kitchen was shut, the staff were cleaning down, the day was over. Perfectly ordinary in hospitality.

Bruno, however, treated it like a civil rights violation. Within minutes he was online posting about the 'shocking service', and before long the post was doing the rounds on social media. By the next morning the café had collected dozens of one-star Google reviews from people who had never set foot in the place, but felt morally compelled to participate in the outrage.

Inside Bruno's head, he's holding businesses accountable. From the other side of the counter it looks slightly different. The owner refreshes the page and watches a rating and a reputation built over years of early mornings, burnt fingers and rent payments slide down because someone turned up after the lights were off.

A minor inconvenience upgraded into a public tribunal, a small business turned into a digital crime scene, all because Bruno discovered that the star system isn't just feedback. It's a weapon with excellent Wi-Fi.

HOW WE PERFORM AND PUNISH — HASHTAG BRUNO

If there is one place cunts in the wild really flourish, it's online. Social media didn't invent the human urge to perform. It just handed everyone a stage, a microphone and some surprisingly competent video-editing tools. Before this, if you were a bit of a show-off you mostly annoyed your friends at dinner. Now you can annoy several thousand strangers before breakfast.

Your breakfast is content. Your gym session is content. Your argument with your partner is content. Your meltdown in the car is content. Your 'I just have to be real with you for a second, guys' face is definitely content. And because the algorithm rewards engagement, and engagement rewards drama, suddenly everything in your life has to be either uplifting, devastating or outrageous. 'Had an average day, nothing special happened' is not a post. 'You would not BELIEVE what they did to me' is.

This is where a particular subspecies thrives: TikTok Bruno. The person for whom every interaction, however mundane, is material. They film service workers without consent to show 'what I had to deal with today'. They livestream their kids' tantrums for laughs. They arrive at disaster sites and pose for concerned selfies they rehearsed in the bathroom mirror. The phone is always out, because at any moment life might hand them a starring role.

The real performance begins when Bruno feels wronged. Private disagreements become 'story time' videos. Ex-partners, ex-friends and ex-colleagues are transformed into villains in a multi-episode narrative arc. Followers are invited to 'do their thing', which is influencer shorthand for go and make this person's life miserable on my behalf. Bruno once had to light a fire adjacent to the neighbour's fence to escalate a dispute. This version does it with a ring light and a 'like, share, comment if you've ever experienced this energy.'

A disturbingly deluxe edition of the same performance appeared in Sydney when a woman posted on Facebook accusing a man in her community of stalking and harassing women. The post spread quickly through local groups. People who had never met the man felt entirely comfortable analysing his character, sharing the allegation and adding their own commentary. His name circulated, the accusation hardened into fact in the comment section, and his reputation began to disintegrate in real time. When the matter eventually reached court, the judge found the claims were false and awarded the man $35,000 in defamation damages, a tidy legal reminder that the internet is not actually a courtroom.

Bruno with a ring light and a social media account.

HOW WE PROTEST — BRUNO WITH A CAUSE

Protest is one of the best things humans do. People standing together to say, *this isn't good enough*, is pretty much the only reason half the rights we take for granted exist at all. Workers marched for fair pay. Women marched for the vote. Civil rights movements marched so entire populations could be treated like actual citizens. There is nothing inherently cunty about marching, chanting or waving a sign.

But protest, like anything that involves attention and moral certainty, is also a magnet for Brunos who aren't that interested in solutions so much as they are interested in being outraged in public. The everyday version is the person who screams abuse at nurses crossing a picket line after a twelve-hour shift, or spits on commuters for not joining their blockade, as if 'wrong place, wrong time' is a moral failure. In their mind the cause is so righteous that anyone not actively applauding must be part of the problem.

The deluxe edition appeared in Sydney in 2022, when a young climate protester climbed onto the Sydney Harbour Bridge during peak hour, lit a flare and sat there while traffic across one of the busiest arteries in the country ground to a halt. The protest was about climate change, a serious issue with plenty of legitimate debate. But for the thousands of people trapped in their cars that morning, the immediate reality was simpler: they were late for work because someone had decided the bridge was now a stage.

Inside her head, she was forcing the nation to confront an existential crisis. From the outside it looked like a protest turning into a performance while ambulances, tradies, nurses and everyone else sat in traffic wondering how exactly this was helping the planet. The courts eventually stepped in, handing down a 15-month prison sentence (later reduced on appeal) – a reminder that while protest is a democratic right, shutting down the Harbour Bridge with a flare tends to move you fairly quickly from activist to headline.

Bruno with Placard.

WHY THIS MATTERS (AND WHY IT'S UNCOMFORTABLE)

It's comforting to think cunts are rare. That they live in history books, court reports and comment sections, not in your own habits. That's a nice story. It's also bullshit.

Every time you or I treat a service worker like an emotional garbage bin, humiliate a colleague to save face, lead a prospective romantic partner on in order to sleep with them, drive like other people don't exist, turn a small shared problem into a multi-year feud, mine someone else's pain for content, weaponise a protest or a review, or escalate a disagreement into a crusade because it makes us feel righteous - we're not doing something completely different from Bruno. We're just doing a smaller, more socially acceptable version.

When nobody's watching except the people who have to live with you, when you're tired, when you're inconvenienced, when you're sure you're right - who are you actually behaving like?

If the answer, more often than not, is 'Bruno, but with better grammar and no Harley', then you're not just a cunt in the wild. You're in the driver's seat.

5

GREED IS GOOD (UNTIL IT ISN'T)

It's satisfying to spot a cunt in the wild. It lets you feel like David Attenborough with more swearing. But if all you ever do is point at other people, you miss the larger, uglier thing that's been going on. Because when enough people, in enough places, are quietly making the same move then you're not just dealing with a few bad eggs. You're dealing with a culture that's been training everyone, including you, to see greed as common sense.

You don't get to this point overnight. We didn't wake up one morning in a society where it is considered perfectly normal to treat a latte mistake like a hate crime, or to see every patch of grass as a legal argument waiting to happen. It happens by degrees. First you're told you're special. Not just as a child. As a customer, as a 'guest', as a user, as a 'valued member'. Every brand is whispering that your preferences are sacred. Streaming services draw up personalised lists just for you. Apps nudge you to 'curate your experience'. Supermarkets run ads about 'Your Way'. It's all very flattering.

Then you're told, in slightly less soothing tones, that the world is harsh. Housing is brutal, jobs are precarious, pensions are for boomers, politics is broken, the planet's on fire, and the only idiot who's going to look out for you is staring at you from the bathroom mirror. That's less flattering, but it lands, because on some level you know it's true. Put those together – 'you are very important' and 'you are on your own' – and you have the perfect compost for a certain kind of greed. Not the cartoon villain hoarding gold in a cave. The respectable, stressed, middle-class version. The one who says, perfectly calmly, 'I don't want to be a cunt ... but I'm not going to be a mug either,' and then proceeds to be a cunt with excellent justification.

THE BACKGROUND DEAL

It's one of the great contradictions of modern life: finance bros rake in six-figure bonuses for shifting numbers across a screen, while teachers, nurses, and frontline workers scrape just to stay afloat in the very communities they hold together. The imbalance isn't subtle, it's blinding. Now, let's be clear, there's nothing wrong with making money. Opportunity is the bedrock of a healthy society, where people feel they can improve their own lives and those of the people they love. But here's the thing: that sense of opportunity is slipping away.

The people teaching our kids, watching over hospital wards at 3 a.m., and keeping the lights on are scrolling through rental listings, realising they can afford roughly one per cent of what's on offer. Meanwhile, the folks moving money from one column to another are deciding whether their bonus covers a beach house or just the Tesla upgrade. You don't need an economics PhD to know something's off when hedge-fund analysts can live within walking distance of public schools, but the teachers inside them can't.

Across most of the affluent Western world, the background deal has shifted. For a while, the story went like this. If you work hard, play moderately fair and don't set too many things on fire, you will, eventually, be allowed some basic stability. A home you don't have to fight for every twelve months. A job that doesn't feel like a permanently collapsing mineshaft. A neighbourhood that, while imperfect, is at least partly recognisable from one decade to the next. That story was never true for everyone, but it was true for enough people that it held. It gave a shape to 'normal life'. It tied your self-interest to a sense that maybe, just maybe, you and your neighbours were in this together.

Now that story has been punched in the face. In city after city, the numbers have gone from 'it's a stretch but doable' to 'are you fucking kidding me?'. Where a modest home once cost three or four times an average annual income, double-digit price-to-income ratios are now treated as normal, even respectable. Young people don't daydream about a house; they run calculators and get the existential dread of a maths teacher. 'Work hard and you'll get there' starts to sound less like encouragement and more like a threat.

WHEN WORK STOPS PAYING

At the same time, the work that used to lock in the dream has gone wobbly. Permanent jobs turn into contracts. Contracts turn into gigs. Wages bump along the bottom while housing, healthcare, education and basic services quietly climb the stairs. You can be the nurse who kept a hospital running through a pandemic and still not be able to afford a one-bedroom flat anywhere near it.

You can be the teacher holding thirty kids' attention on a Friday afternoon and still be told that 'the market' says you should live two hours away and commute. Meanwhile, at the top, executives and senior managers discover that 'performance-based incentives' means their bonuses balloon five, ten, a hundred times faster than the pay of the people whose names they don't know.

Layer on top of that the cultural churn, migration reshaping suburbs, social norms shifting faster than a lot of people's nervous systems, technology rearranging how we talk, shop, date, fight and work. For some, that's overdue and liberating. For others, it feels like waking up in a house where someone has moved all your furniture and then called you a bigot when you trip over the coffee table. It is not surprising, in that context, that people start grabbing. If you feel like the game is rigged and the rules change every election cycle, 'look after number one' stops feeling like a selfish motto and starts feeling like basic survival.

OFFICE GREED

Workplaces aren't much better. Walk into a modern office and you'll see values posters, wellbeing initiatives, diversity committees and maybe even a mindfulness app subsidised by HR. Underneath, the actual operating instructions are simple. Hit your targets, cut your costs, don't embarrass anyone important.

In that environment, greed doesn't have to be spectacular. It just has to sit there while people quietly trade away everything that isn't measured. You keep the star salesperson who abuses staff because they 'bring in the numbers'. You restructure three jobs into one and call it 'efficiency', then blink in amazement when the person in the remaining chair ends up burnt out and bitter. You talk about 'our people' and mean 'our people whose metrics are green'.

Again, nobody wakes up planning to be a cunt. In their own narrative they're simply the person making the tough decisions. They go home and tell their friends, 'Look, I hate doing it, but it's my job.' They learn not to think too hard about the junior who started the year enthusiastic and is now googling 'signs of burnout' in the office bathroom. The company keeps inching towards a culture where everyone is slightly afraid and slightly resentful, and where the only people who thrive are those most willing to weaponise their own self-interest and call it performance.

It works the other way too. Staff watch organisations drop people they've worked with for years to protect a quarterly result and quietly recalibrate their own loyalty. Why would you stay late, go the extra mile or stick your neck out if you've just seen how that plays out for the last person who tried? You become more transactional because you'd feel stupid not to. You might not be exploiting anyone, but you've joined the same game. Minimum in, maximum out, don't get attached. In a world like that, greed doesn't just slip through the cracks; it builds extensions.

THE PROPERTY LADDER AND THE MOAT

The trouble is that greed doesn't just move into that gap. It turns it into a moat. It starts small, with sensible-sounding thoughts. I should make sure my family is safe. I should get some security. I shouldn't be naive. I shouldn't rely on anyone else. All fine. All true. Then it quietly shifts the goalposts. You're not just trying to keep your head above water; you're building a little viewing platform from which to shout about all the people who can't swim.

You see this very clearly in the property game. At first, buying a home is about not being at the mercy of a landlord. Fair. Then it's about 'making your money work for you'. Then it's a second place, 'just as an investment'. Then it's voting against anything that might give other people the same chance you had, because it might shave a percent off your gains. Change the zoning so more housing can be built? Absolutely not. It will ruin the character of a suburb you moved into six years ago. Give renters more security? That's an attack on 'mum and dad investors', who are somehow both vulnerable and entirely responsible for the national housing stock shortages.

Everyone has a story. We did it tough too. Nobody helped us. Interest rates were higher back then. Kids these days want everything at once. Stop eating avocado toast. The details vary but the shape is always the same. Whatever makes your pile bigger is prudent; whatever threatens it is outrageous. It's amazing how fast 'don't be a cunt' turns into 'don't be a mug' once the numbers get big enough.

It's the same logic that lets us nod along while essential workers are priced out of the cities they keep alive, so long as the median price of our house keeps climbing and our super looks healthy. We tell ourselves, 'Of course nurses and teachers should be paid more, of course they should live closer to work,' and then quietly vote down anything that might nudge our rates or tax bracket or property portfolio. We clap for them in a crisis, then go back to designing systems where their reward for holding society together is a longer commute and a worse rental. Greed doesn't always look like a villain cackling over piles of cash; often, it looks like an otherwise decent person who has decided that as long as their family is 'secure', everyone else can be a line item for the government to sort out later.

Strata and homeowners' associations are like laboratory dishes for this stuff. On paper, they're gorgeous little experiments in cooperation. You and a bunch of strangers share walls, roofs, pipes and garden beds. You pool money to look after the shared bits. You agree on some rules so nobody turns the foyer into a carport or the hallway into a kennel. It's everyday democracy in trackpants.

Then greed shows up in slippers and calls itself 'common sense'. Nobody wants levies to go up, so essential maintenance is postponed. 'One more year, we'll sort it next time.' Next time becomes ten years. Roofs leak, concrete rusts, waterproofing fails. Everyone insists they're being responsible, 'people can't afford big increases right now'. Future owners, including older versions of themselves, can apparently afford to live in a slowly disintegrating building, so that's fine.

On the ground, you get the 'my lot' philosophers. The person who decides the strip of common garden outside their window is 'basically mine' and rips it up for a private veggie patch. The person who blocks necessary works because the scaffolding might slightly affect their tenant's view for a month. The amateur electrician who wires their private spa into common power. Call them on it and they don't say, 'Yes, I'm undermining the shared asset for my convenience.' They say, 'Why are you making such a big deal? I pay my levies. I've worked hard. It's my property too.' Tiny acts of respectable greed, one after another, until the whole building is one big argument about money trapped in concrete.

From the outside, it's a textbook 'tragedy of the commons'. From the inside, it's fifty people insisting they're just looking out for themselves while quietly making life more expensive and more hostile for everyone in the postcode.

THE LANGUAGE OF SELF-INTEREST

In housing, in work, in neighbourhoods, in politics, the story about shared progress frays. People feel unmoored and under threat. Greed steps forward and offers a simpler story: look after your own.

You can hear it in the way people talk. A lot of sentences now start with 'I'm all for X, but...' and end with 'as long as it doesn't affect me'. I'm all for more housing, but not if it changes my street. I'm all for fair wages, but not if it means prices go up. I'm all for multiculturalism, but not if I have to hear other languages on the train. I'm all for refugees, but I don't have any room in my rented apartment to house them. I'm all for reform, but not if it means my taxes, my suburb, my comfort take the hit.

Do you vote down the roof replacement because you might not be living here in five years? Do you underpay the cleaner because you know she won't argue? Do you let the star manager keep kicking down because they keep kicking the numbers up? Do you support that policy because it genuinely seems fair, or because it keeps your unearned gains safely insulated from other people's needs?

This isn't about guilt. Guilt is just another story you can drown in. This is about clarity. Greed thrives in foggy thinking. It wants you to believe that your choices are either irrelevant or inevitable. They're neither. They're small, cumulative and consequential.

SELF-INTEREST WITHOUT BECOMING BRUNO

So where does that leave self-interest? Are you supposed to throw yourself on the altar of the common good every time someone waves a banner? No. That would be ridiculous. Pure selflessness is about as realistic as pure evil. Understandably, you are going to care more about your family than about strangers. You are going to worry more about your bills than about global capital flows. You are going to feel your own losses more keenly than other people's. That's not failure. That's being an organism. The question is not 'Do you care about yourself?'

It's 'Can you care about yourself in a way that doesn't quietly turn you into Bruno with a mortgage?'

Grown-up self-interest has some basic features. It can think beyond this quarter, this election cycle, this tantrum. It can recognise that making everything someone else's problem is a short-term win and a long-term mess. It can sit with the discomfort of 'this costs me a bit now, but it stops everything costing me a lot later'. It can tolerate the idea that sometimes you will be the one who backs down, pays more, gives ground, and that this does not automatically make you a mug – it makes you someone who understands that you live in a network, not a vacuum.

Self-interest also has a sense of humour about itself. It can spot, in real time, when the internal monologue 'I'm just being sensible' has shifted into 'I'm going to fuck over everyone else in this room and pretend I had no option'. It can laugh, a little, at the part of you that wants to be the hero of every story, and instead aim for something less glamorous. Not making things worse unnecessarily. Greed will always be there, whispering its lies.

You've earned this. They don't deserve that. The system is rigged. You'd be an idiot not to. Everyone else would do the same. Sometimes it will be right. Often it will be almost right, which is more dangerous. The trick, if there is one, is not to silence that voice - you can't - but to add another one. A small, stubborn, slightly older voice that asks, 'Okay, and then what?' Not just for you, but for the people who share your building, your workplace, your city, your country. The people whose names you don't know but whose lives are quietly shaped by your decisions, as yours are by theirs.

6

THE LAW REFLECTS US

By the time you've normalised a bit of everyday cuntishness in how you shop, drive, work and live, it's only a matter of time before some faceless cunt in a suit decides to write it down and turn it into policy. Individual habits don't stay individual for long. They leak upwards. The logic that governs the shopping centre car park eventually finds its way into parliaments, departments and courtrooms.

LAW AS A MIRROR

The law is supposed to reflect a society's values and protect it. Most of the time it simply mirrors it. When a society grows anxious, greedy and a little cunty, the law does not sit there like a serene old judge dispensing wisdom. It flinches. It tightens. It panics. Then it solemnly informs everyone that the new restrictions are entirely for their own protection.

We like to imagine the law as something above us, carved in stone, handed down in Latin, noble and neutral. In reality, most of what ends up on the statute books is just our day-to-day neuroses with a coat of parliamentary paint. How we complain, how we punish, how we hoard, how we avoid discomfort eventually get written down, weaponised and enforced.

The small decisions we normalise in cafés, cars and committees grow up, move to the capital and start limiting what we can say, build, think and do. And sometimes it happens quicker than we imagine. When horror strikes, it rewrites laws. But horror never lands in clear air. It blows into a climate that is already thick.

Politicians, for their part, rarely invent these moods. They harvest them. Anxiety becomes a press conference. Outrage becomes a bill. Fear becomes a new power that will definitely only be used in the most exceptional circumstances, circumstances that somehow keep occurring every few months. The uncomfortable truth is that the vast majority of modern politicians bear little resemblance to the statesmen and stateswomen we like to imagine from the past.

Too many are themselves products of the same anxious culture they claim to lead: neurotic, media-trained, occasionally narcissistic and highly attuned to the emotional temperature of the crowd. Their instinct is rarely to steady a frightened public but to surf it. They play to the popular rather than the difficult, to the applause line rather than the hard truth. The long, dull work of leadership – explaining limits, absorbing anger and telling voters things they do not want to hear – is far less attractive than the short-term reward of appearing decisive in front of a camera. And when the next shock arrives, the machinery is already warmed up.

BEFORE BONDI

Before the Bondi terror attack in December 2025, antisemitism had been humming away in the background for years. After 7 October 2023, it changed key. Hamas' massacre in southern Israel that day, a level of antisemitic violence not seen in decades, left around 1,200 people murdered and more than 250 taken hostage. Entire families were butchered in their homes, at a music festival and on quiet rural streets. It was the grim full stop at the end of a decade of warnings that many people preferred not to hear.

Many of those marching in cities around Australia and the rest of the World, draped in the keffiyeh, waving Palestinian flags and shouting 'from the river to the sea, Palestine will be free', argue that 7 October did not happen in a vacuum. They point to the long history of Palestinian dispossession, the occupation of the West Bank, the blockade of Gaza and the daily reality of life under a conflict that has ground on for generations. On that point their argument has merit.

Conflicts like this do not appear out of thin air. Entire families in the region have lived through war after war, and the devastation that followed Israel's military response has brought extraordinary human suffering and loss on a scale that for many Palestinians feels like their own catastrophe, 'the Nakba' replayed. Images of bombed neighbourhoods, children pulled from rubble and people queuing for water and food are not propaganda. You would have to be numb not to feel something for people trapped inside that kind of suffering. But history cuts in more than one direction.

Israel withdrew its settlements and permanent military presence from Gaza in 2005. The following year, Gazans elected Hamas, a movement committed to Israel's destruction and to armed struggle as its central strategy. What followed was not peace but another cycle of violence:

rockets fired into Israeli towns, Israeli military retaliation, tightening restrictions on Gaza and repeated wars that have left civilians on both sides living under the shadow of conflict.

None of that erases Palestinian suffering. But neither does it make the deliberate massacre of civilians any less monstrous. Understanding the history of a conflict is not the same thing as excusing atrocities committed in its name. What matters here is not adjudicating every grievance of the Middle East in a few paragraphs. What matters is what happened next.

ANTI-SEMITISM VS PALESTINIAN SOLIDARITY

Since 7 October, and alongside the Israeli government's military response in Gaza, Jews in Australia and across the world have carried a double weight: grief for Israelis murdered or taken hostage, and a sharp rise in antisemitic hostility in the places where they themselves live. Reports from community security groups, Jewish organisations and governments tell roughly the same story. In the months and years following the 7 October attack, antisemitic incidents surged to record or near-record levels in many countries, including Australia. Jews who had long assumed they were living in stable liberal democracies suddenly found themselves looking over their shoulders again.

Some of it wore the old clothes. Mutters about Jewish power. Stars of David graffitied on synagogue walls that made the news for one cycle before being quietly filed away as 'a bit sad'. But some of it arrived wrapped in something else: genuine outrage about what was happening in Gaza and the West Bank. Painful images circulated endlessly across phones and televisions, families bombed out of their homes, bodies carried through shattered streets, desperate crowds searching for food and water. That suffering was real. It still is.

I am of Lebanese descent, with close Palestinian and Jewish friends, and years watching my country of origin be used as a battlefield for other people's ambitions. That history strips away romantic illusions about any of the region's armed actors - and it changes nothing about what follows.

That is the point. Having reasons to resent the political actors of the Middle East does not cancel basic humanity when confronted with the death and destruction they inflict on civilians. It is possible to loathe the politics and still grieve for a child under the rubble, whether that child is in Gaza, Tel Aviv or Beirut. Just as it is possible to be horrified by a shooting at Bondi without turning the victims into props for a favourite culture war script.

If an ideology requires empathy to be switched off, if it demands that dead strangers be treated as acceptable collateral because they belong to the wrong tribe, then whatever else it claims to be doing, it is not defending justice. It is simply looking for a new excuse to be a cunt. This is not a competition in suffering. It is not a debate about who is more morally justified.

You can acknowledge that Palestinians have been brutalised without turning that grief into a permission slip to menace Jews in Sydney. You can be horrified by families obliterated overseas and still say, without hesitation, that a father and son walking onto a beach with rifles and murdering sixteen people celebrating Hanukkah is not 'resistance' in the name of Islam. They are butchers.

What poisoned the air here was the way those two streams of pain began to be thrown at each other like weapons. Criticism of a government blurred into hostility towards a people. Solidarity with Palestinians blurred into intimidation of Jewish kids on buses and outside schools. Chants that might mean one thing in a distant conflict began to sound very different when they were shouted outside a synagogue or a Jewish day school.

Jewish Australians did what Jews everywhere do when history clears its throat. They took note. They changed routes to shul. They briefed their children on what to do if someone started filming them in the street. They watched as respectable voices minimised the rising hostility as 'just tension' or 'strong feelings on both sides'. The message was familiar. You are, once again, on your own.

Then came Bondi.

THE BONDI ATROCITY

It was supposed to be the opposite of a threat. A public Hanukkah gathering on a famous beach, candles in the dusk, kids kicking foam balls in the shallows, songs drifting over the sound of waves and buses. The whole point was to inhabit public space openly, to say, 'We are here, we belong, we're not hiding.'

A father and son turned up with high-powered rifles and an ISIS flag. Not a keyboard warrior. Not a nasty chant. Two men who looked at a scene of lights and kids and plastic chairs and decided it was the stage for their holy war fantasy. They walked past the fairy lights and opened fire. Sixteen people died on sand that had been raked that afternoon, on a beach that has been sold for decades as the country's soft, safe, sun-bleached heart.

The footage showed beachgoers sprinting in thongs, tourists pressed flat behind concrete walls, bodies half in the shallows, half on the beach. Bondi isn't abstract. It's on postcards, tourism campaigns, smug sunrise selfies. Watching it turned into a killing field felt like seeing the national screensaver shot to pieces.

For Jewish Australians, the message was brutally direct: the thing you quietly feared is absolutely possible here. For everyone else, it punctured the comforting story that this sort of thing happens in other countries, to other people, in places with 'issues'. Now it was between the flags. When horror hits like that, the emotional demand is simple and loud. Protect us. Do something. Make sure this never happens again. And in a country without an enshrined right to free speech, that demand has a very short path to the statute book.

THE PANIC BILL

In the weeks that followed, thousands rightfully mourned. Candles in paper cups lined the promenade. Messages and wreaths piled up on the railings and at the spots on the beach where people had fallen. Politicians queued for the microphones, faces set to sombre, heads bowed under borrowed yarmulkes, talking about 'our Jewish brothers and sisters', 'an attack on all of us', 'evil on our shores'.

For a brief moment, the usual partisan sniping died down. Parliament was recalled. 'Emergency' became the magic password. Late-night sittings. Urgent briefings. Closed-door meetings. Protests were banned 'out of respect' and 'to prevent further division'. Public squares were cleared. Permits quietly refused. The subtext was: feel what you like, but don't bring your feelings to the street right now.

And in that atmosphere, a hefty hate speech bill rocketed from the shadows to centre stage. It was waved around as a moral necessity, a line in the sand, a promise that if bullets hadn't stopped this, the law would. Here, the lived experience of bureaucracy matters. Having worked in government and dealt directly with the machinery, I can unashamedly say there is no way a piece of legislation of that size and complexity was dreamed up, drafted from scratch and prepped for tabling in the few frantic days after the Bondi massacre, especially heading into the summer shutdown period, when half of Canberra was already on a beach somewhere else.

Even in normal times, a bill like that would expect months of gestation, policy development, exposure drafts, committee hearings, submissions, internal brawls, redrafts. It would snake through procedures, working groups, 'stakeholder engagement' and the ritual theatre of scrutiny before anyone stood up to move the first reading. Yet here it was, dense, far-reaching, ready to go, while the blood on the sand was barely dry. I am not a conspiracy theorist. I would rather not speculate about which think tank, department or ministerial office had this tucked in a drawer waiting for a suitable outrage to ride in on.

In the end, it doesn't really matter who sharpened the pencil. What matters is the outcome, a law that, under the banner of protecting us from hate, effectively narrowed who we can be as individuals and as a society. When it finally staggered out of that late-night Senate vote, it didn't land like some neat, bipartisan 'we did the right thing' moment. It landed like a brick in a crowded pool. Jewish groups, human rights lawyers, civil libertarians, party hacks and columnists all started thrashing in different directions, some insisting it didn't go far enough, others insisting it went way too far, and a talented few managing to argue both in the same sentence.

The government's sales pitch hardened overnight. This was now 'the toughest hate-speech framework' the country had ever seen, proof they were cracking down on hate groups, extremists and anyone who thought it was clever to menace vulnerable communities. Visa powers, 'prohibited hate group' labels, new offences and heavier penalties were paraded as evidence that something serious had been done.

Many Jewish organisations, who had been watching the temperature rise for years, welcomed it with gritted teeth. It wasn't everything some had wanted, and bits of the original draft had been watered down or ripped out to get it through, but compared with the nothing they'd been offered for a long time, it was something. When you've just watched your safest beach become a crime scene, 'something' can feel like oxygen.

Human rights and refugee advocates stared at the same pages and saw something else: a rushed law, vague definitions, big new sticks in the hands of ministers and security agencies, and a lot of blind faith that future governments will always be wise and kind. For them, a bill that was sold as a shield for Jews and other minorities also looked uncomfortably like a sword aimed at protesters, migrants and anyone who might end up on the wrong side of a 'hate group' list.

Civil-liberty types and a decent handful of academics chimed in with the usual boring, absolutely necessary warning: laws drafted in the heat of grief tend to age badly. They talked about 'chilling effects' on protest and political speech, about platforms and employers overcomplying rather than risking a test case, about how seriousness of purpose isn't the same thing as precision of drafting.

Inside politics, it tidied nothing up. The government claimed a national security win and posed as the adults in the room. The opposition tied itself in knots trying to be tough on antisemitism and extremism without looking like it had signed away its free speech credibility. The Greens and chunks of the crossbench pointed proudly to the nastiest bits they'd forced out, and kept campaigning against the nastiness that remained. Everyone walked out of the chamber claiming to have saved the country from someone else's excess.

Out in the world, the law did what laws always do: it started to sink into the societal fabric. Departments drew up flow charts. Agencies wrote guidance notes. Community 'stakeholder' briefings were scheduled. Law-and-order commentators demanded the first big scalp to prove it all meant something. Activists on every side re-tooled their talking points. Ordinary people quietly tried to work out whether the chant, tweet, sermon, placard or angry email they were thinking about had just crept closer to a tripwire.

RIGHTS WITHOUT A GUARDRAIL

Unlike in the United States, Australia does not have a bold First Amendment we can wave as a hard stop. Our most important protection for speech, the implied freedom of political communication, lives in High Court judgments and constitutional convention. It is real, but it is not a big, simple sentence at the front of the Constitution that everyone knows. It is the sort of protection that requires calm weather and careful argument to defend. Bondi gave us the opposite.

In that storm, the hate-speech bill sailed through. On the surface it targeted the worst of the worst: neo-Nazis, jihadist fanboys, anyone who thinks it is clever to chant for genocide outside places where Jews live, pray or study. In practice, it did what panic-drafted laws usually do: it drew the net wider.

Incitement to violence was already illegal. This went further. It created broad offences around speech that could be interpreted as stirring up hatred, contempt or serious ridicule of protected groups. 'Hate' stopped meaning 'you are vermin, you should die' and drifted towards anything that might make someone feel less safe or less valued.

Most people heard: we're finally cracking down on the worst nuts. What the text quietly said was this: we now have a bigger stick labelled 'Hate', and we will decide when you are holding it.

And if history teaches anything, it's that once a government has a bigger stick, some bored bureaucrat or ambitious politician will find a way to swing it at the wrong cunt.

FEAR'S STORY ABOUT SPEECH

This is how fear short-circuits rights. The story we tell ourselves is neat: rising hateful speech creates a climate of hatred, that climate makes violence more likely, and if we throttle the speech we throttle the violence.

There is some truth in that sequence. Language can prepare the soil for violence. Normalising talk of extermination and conspiracy makes it easier for unstable people to see neighbours as targets. Any Jewish person who has watched old slurs crawl back into daylight knows words are not harmless.

But in the rush to be seen to do something, we flatten all the speech we dislike into the same bucket: dangerous. We stretch the idea of harm until it covers not just direct incitement and dehumanisation, but abrasive criticism, unpopular theology, harsh jokes and political opinions that make people's skin crawl.

We start writing law for vibes. Without a hard constitutional guardrail saying you cannot go past this point, rights live or die by ordinary legislation. The same parliament that gives you a public holiday can quietly carve away the territory in which you are allowed to argue about what that holiday means.

That is how you move, in a fortnight, from standing with your Jewish community, which is right, to making certain public speech illegal. And because the definitions are elastic, the people deciding what counts as hate today might not be the same people deciding tomorrow, and some of them will absolutely be cunts.

THE LANGUAGE PROBLEM

If this were happening in a culture that loved patient, honest speech, you might hope the rough edges would be sanded down over time. But we are trying to do it with a public language that has already been hollowed out. We talk endlessly about inclusion, respect, safety and dignity. They are good words. The problem is how often they are used as fig leaves for control. For example:

- Inclusive starts to mean 'only people who agree with us'.
- Respectful starts to mean 'never question certain ideas'.
- Safe becomes 'nothing that upsets me is allowed near me'.

Our feeds train us to speak in declarations, condemnations and performative concern, not in careful argument. Social media sells us a double hit of false happiness, moral superiority and consumer lust. We get to feel both outraged and fabulous – neither of which helps us live with people we dislike.

Lawmakers, regulators and corporate boards swim in that same water. They see who gets dog-piled and who gets applause. They learn very quickly that you get punished for defending unpopular freedoms and rewarded for stamping your foot about harm in the vaguest possible terms.

In that environment, it is much easier to pass a broad law against hate and let some future tribunal worry about the details than to stand up during national mourning and say: 'We need to be careful about speech, even now.' Because that sort of sentence does not trend well online, and no politician enjoys discovering that half the internet thinks they are defending the rights of cunts.

THE BUREAUCRATIC LOOP

Add bureaucracy and the system becomes self-feeding. New laws create new work, new work justifies new units, and new units require new data, reporting and intervention. Departments and agencies are not monsters. They are living organisms — and in some cases parasites. They monitor, accredit, approve and investigate. Their product is process; their food is your money. Once created, they want to survive. Once they survive, they want to grow.

A hate-speech law like this is a buffet. Guidelines must be written. Training rolled out. Monitoring systems purchased. Hotlines staffed. Community engagement strategies launched. Every new outrage — another clip, another chant, another idiot with a placard — becomes evidence that the system must expand further.

At street level, you see a few high-profile prosecutions of genuine extremists and think it's good. In the long tail, you see something quieter: protests squeezed into narrower channels, campus debates wrapped in codes of conduct, platforms over-enforcing out of an abundance of caution, employers disciplining staff for legal speech outside work because it might upset a client.

You do not stop being allowed to talk. You simply start asking yourself whether it is worth the potential paperwork, the possible complaint, the HR meeting, the regulator's email, or the professional busybody who decides to make themselves the official reporting officer for other people's opinions. Every society eventually breeds a few of those cunts.

FENCE OR NET?

None of this is an argument for shrugging at real hatred or real danger. A society that cannot protect Jews on a beach, Muslims at prayer, Christians in a church, women walking home, migrants finishing a late shift is not free; it is failing. The law does have a job here: drawing hard, narrow lines around threats and incitement to violence. But there is a difference between a fence around the worst behaviour and a net thrown over everyone.

The way we are drifting, each fresh atrocity becomes a reason to tighten the net. A little less speech. A little more monitoring. A little less protest. A little more process. Taken alone, each step can be defended. Taken together, they quietly change the air.

THE PRICE OF STAYING FREE

In reality, the law reflects us. Right now, it reflects a society that is scared, angry and tempted to trade messy freedoms for the illusion of perfect safety. It reflects our better instincts – solidarity after atrocity, compassion for communities under attack – and our worse ones. The desire to shut each other up. To outsource difficult conversations to regulators. To tidy away people we dislike rather than learning how to live with them. You do not let raw emotion drive lawmaking and then act surprised when the law itself turns out raw.

If we want something better, it will not be enough to shout free speech when our tribe is under pressure and demand bans when someone else opens their mouth. It will mean defending principles even when they shelter people we cannot stand. It will mean accepting that offence, risk and the occasional truly awful opinion are part of the price of not living under permanent supervision.

Because every time we cheer a law that clamps down on them, we teach the system how to clamp down on us. And by the time it does, the law will simply be reflecting what we taught it: that whenever some cunt hurts us, we would rather tighten the leash than risk being free.

7

UTOPIAN CUNTS – THE DEATH OF THE CENTRE

For more than a hundred years, the political extremes have been selling versions of the same fantasy. On the left, the dream is socialism and eventually communism finally done properly, a world where nobody is exploited, wealth is shared and justice rolls over like a Netflix subscription. On the right, the dream is a market so free it floats above human frailty, where regulation is a dirty word, taxes are theft and prosperity trickles down like some kind of benevolent golden shower from the heights of capital.

Each side swears that if we just give them enough power and enough time to deal with the idiots and the enemies, they can deliver utopia. Each side promises freedom and dignity. Each side, in practice, has a track record of concentrating power and wealth in the hands of a very small group of cunts while telling everyone else that this, somehow, is liberation.

THE SILENT MIRACLE

In the middle of the twentieth century, most western democracies quietly did something much less glamorous and much more effective. They built mixed economies. Governments taxed progressively, ran public schools and hospitals, funded safety nets and pensions. Markets allocated many resources, but not all. Trade unions and businesses actually endeavoured to sit at the same table and negotiate. People believed, not always wrongly, that their kids might be better off than they were.

These societies were not pure, and they were not fair to everyone, particularly anyone outside the old default of straight, white and male, but for a while they managed something rare in human history. They were very rich and, by historical standards, surprisingly egalitarian. That is an astonishing achievement if you stop doomscrolling long enough to notice it. For most of human history, the normal shape of society was a very fat bottom and a very pointy top: peasants, serfs and servants at one end, a tiny cluster of people with titles, land or guns at the other. The middle was a rumour.

In the decades after the Second World War, approximately from 1950 to the year 2000, in a handful of countries, we built something closer to a diamond, a thick, confident middle who owned homes, took holidays and expected their kids to go further. We did that not by picking an extreme, but by muddling through the centre, combining markets with public goods, individual freedom with shared responsibility, argument with compromise. Then, quickly, we became bored, offended, impatient and certain. The messy centre that had delivered the goods began to look, to activists and ideologues on both sides, less like a hard-won sacrifice through compromise and more like a betrayal.

That is the moment the utopian cunts smelt opportunity.

The problem is not just the politicians or the billionaire donors. It is you, it is me, it is anyone who would rather chant a simple slogan than live with a complicated compromise. Purity feels better than trade-offs. Being absolutely right feels better than being partly right and partly unsure. Once you are hooked on that feeling, the boring arithmetic of who gets what, who loses what and what happens if this policy sticks around for twenty years feels beneath you. You do not want a budget; you want a cleansing.

EQUALITY AT GUNPOINT — WHEN THE LEFT GOES PERFECT

The revolutionary left tells a story about history with one simple plot: you are oppressed, and we can fix it. In this script, the economy is a rigged game where bosses and owners live off the stolen labour of workers. The answer is not to regulate, redistribute or restrain; it is to overturn. Put the means of production into collective hands. Replace messy parliaments with a vanguard that truly understands the dialectic. Sweep aside the old elites and build a classless society where nobody starves and nobody owns anyone else.

On paper, it is intoxicating. If you grew up poor, overlooked, or discriminated against - particularly as someone intellectually inclined - there's a quiet bitterness in watching less educated or capable people achieve financial success through risk-taking, while you remain in a modest academic or bureaucratic role. As you struggle with rent consuming your income, and witness others casually acquiring their third waterfront property, the contrast becomes more than frustrating - it's intoxicating. It feels like the first honest story you have heard. This is the first trick of utopian cunthood.

Take something real and painful, name it clearly, then smuggle your own entitlement inside the solution. Of course people are sick of being exploited. Of course they are tired of pretending the system is fair when one bloke's 'annual bonus' is more than they will see in a decade. Of course they are angry. The question is what you do with that anger. The revolutionary answer is, give it to us, and stop asking questions.

In practice, the socialist and communist experiments that actually got their hands on state power followed the same three pillars just in a new uniform. Entitlement showed up in the party elite who lived better than everyone else 'for the revolution', with special stores, cars and dachas, while everyone else queued for bread.

It showed up in the assumption that a small group of men with the right pamphlets were entitled to decide the fate of millions because they understood history and you did not. Their time mattered; your life did not. If your village had to starve to prove a point about agricultural policy, that was tragic but necessary, and definitely not their fault.

Cowardice came wrapped in slogans about necessity. No one ordered executions; the line demanded them. No one silenced dissent; history could not be allowed to go backwards. Responsibility dissolved into historical forces, central committees and 'the people', a bland pronoun you could hide anything behind. Once you give people that kind of moral camouflage, you can talk them into almost anything. It is the same move as the guided missile email, just scaled up: I am not being vicious, I am defending a principle.

Cruelty, once unleashed, did what cruelty always does when it has paperwork and guns; it went to work. People disappeared into camps, farms were collectivised badly enough to kill millions, whole professions were purged and neighbours learned to denounce neighbours before someone denounced them first. You did not have to pull a trigger to be part of it. You just had to keep your head down, mouth the slogans and tell yourself that any discomfort you felt was a price worth paying for the radiant future. If you can watch someone lose their job, home and freedom because they disagreed with the party line and still sleep like a baby because the pamphlet says they are class enemies, you are not a freedom fighter. You are a cunt in a beret.

None of this means that every complaint about capitalism is hysteria, or that every person who uses the word socialism is one haircut away from nationalising your corner café. It does mean that any politics which insists there is one correct line, one pure vanguard, and that dissenters are not just wrong but morally filthy, is already flirting with the same three pillars.

The moment your side becomes 'the people' and everyone else becomes enemies of the people, you have handed yourself a licence to do almost anything in the name of justice. You have built your own little utopian freeway and put cunthood in the fast lane.

BLOOD AND SOIL — WHEN THE RIGHT GOES TRIBAL

On the other side of the bonfire stands a different kind of fundamentalist, clutching not a spreadsheet but a flag. In this story, the problem is not exploitation by owners or even interference by the state; the problem is them. The wrong race, the wrong religion, the wrong culture, the wrong newcomers ruining the country that supposedly belonged to you and your grandparents. Taxes, regulations and welfare still get a mention, but mainly as things that are being stolen from the 'real people' and handed to strangers.

The promise here is not endless opportunity; it is restored greatness. We will make the nation pure again, strong again, safe again, great again once we stop apologising to, and pandering to, everyone who is not like us.

Again, it sounds plausible if you have spent years being told that your problems are entirely your fault. When your town has lost its factories, your school feels rougher and poorer, and your rent chews most of your wages, it is very comforting to hear that the reason is not the people at the top who have been rorting the system, but the people at the bottom and on the edges who have supposedly been given too much.

The story starts by naming real pain, lost jobs, frayed communities, a sense that the place you grew up in has changed faster than you can understand. Then it smuggles in its own entitlement under the banner of heritage. Heritage, in this script, quietly means that people who look like you, worship like you and sound like you should have more of a claim on the country than everyone else.

The same three pillars drive the show. Entitlement is the first. It is the belief that the nation is essentially your private inheritance and that others are, at best, guests who should be grateful and quiet. It shows up when someone says 'we' built this country, and the 'we' mysteriously excludes Indigenous people, migrants, the wrong religions and anyone who does not fit the nostalgic postcard.

It shows up when a politician wraps themselves in a flag to argue that certain suburbs, schools or jobs should be reserved for 'our own' first, as if citizenship comes in tiers. Underneath it sits a simple belief: my group's comfort and dominance are normal, and anyone else's presence is a problem to be managed.

Cowardice, as usual, dresses itself up as toughness. Nobody ever says, 'I'm scared of change and confused by difference.' They say, 'I'm just telling it like it is' and 'Someone has to stand up for us.' The targets are always chosen carefully. It is much easier to shout at refugees on a boat than at the minister who signed the contracts that hollowed out your town.

It is easier to rant about the hijab, the mosque or the housing commission estate than to ask why the local hospital ward just closed. Racist cowardice specialises in punching down while pretending to punch up. It calls itself bravery because it is loud, but it is terrified of looking honestly at who actually holds power.

Cruelty here is not a glitch; it is part of the fun. The racist right delights in jokes that dehumanise whole groups in chants and memes that reduce people to animals, criminals or invaders. It shows up when a shock jock talks about 'floods' and 'swarms', when a politician describes asylum seekers as a 'tide', when an online mob piles onto an Indigenous sportsperson or a Muslim teenager with threats and slurs and then insists it was just banter.

It shows up in policies designed less to solve problems than to send messages. Offshore camps in places nobody can see, police powers that mysteriously land hardest on certain skins, welfare rules that treat some families as permanent suspects. If you can look at a child in a cage, a family on a leaking boat, a community being harassed in its own street and feel a secret thrill because 'they' had it coming, you are not defending your culture. You are a cunt with a flag.

The ugliest trick of racist politics is that it offers belonging while quietly stripping it from others. It tells lonely, angry people, 'You are part of something noble and ancient. Your blood and your soil matter.' It offers them a tribe and a story big enough to stand in. But the price of that hug is simple. You must agree that some people are less human than you. Once you accept that, anything becomes thinkable. Deportations, bans, walls, segregated services, casual violence, 'random' checks – all can be justified because you have convinced yourself that the people on the receiving end do not feel things the way you do, or do not deserve safety the way you do.

None of this means that every worry about immigration, culture or social change is racist, or that every person who cares about traditions is one march away from joining a torch-lit rally. It does mean that any politics which constantly defines 'real' citizens in narrower and narrower terms, which treats diversity as contamination and equality as a threat, is already deep in cunthood.

The moment your patriotism depends on someone else being permanently suspect because of how they look, where they came from or how they pray, you have not discovered love of country. You have discovered a socially acceptable way to be a cowardly, entitled, cruel little cunt and call it principle.

WHEN BOTH ROADS LEAD TO THE SAME CLIFF

Back in wealthy democracies, the pattern plays out more politely than in collapsing states, but the shape is the same. The widening gap creates anger, anxiety and resentment. The political extremes step forward and offer simple explanations. The left-wing utopian looks at the inequality and declares capitalism inherently evil. Tear it down. Replace markets with enlightened planning.

Give the right people control of the levers and justice will finally arrive. The blood-and-soil utopian looks at the same problem and reaches the opposite conclusion. The system is fine. The real problem is lazy people, woke elites, immigrants or whichever villain happens to be fashionable this week. Both are, in their own ways, being cunts.

There is a simple test for these ideas. Imagine a society where everyone behaves exactly as the extremists recommend. In the left-wing utopia, private ownership disappears. The state or party allocates housing, appoints your boss and decides what you are allowed to say in public. In the racist right-wing utopia, citizenship quietly splits into two tiers: people like us, who belong fully, and everyone else, who never quite do. Police patrol those lines. Schools and suburbs sort themselves accordingly. The state's job becomes comforting some and containing others.

In both systems, the same thing happens. Small circles with the right connections learn how to manipulate the machinery of power while everyone else learns how to keep their head down. In both systems, questioning the arrangement marks you as suspect, a traitor to the revolution on one side, a traitor to your people on the other. In both systems, the gap between promise and reality is blamed on enemies, saboteurs or human nature, never on the structure itself. If that is not cunthood on a national scale, it is hard to know what is.

The twist extremists rarely mention is that these worlds do not arrive overnight. They arrive slowly. One compromised principle. One ignored abuse. One selfish decision at a time. They arrive every time we reward rage over reason, purity over competence and slogans over boring detail. Every time we ignore the smell coming from our own backyard because our side is supposedly virtuous. Every time a cheap joke about 'them' goes unchallenged. Every time a policy clearly targeting a minority slips past because it 'doesn't affect me'. All of that is easier to pull off in a culture that has quietly stopped training people to notice their own bullshit.

THE SLOW DEATH OF THINKING

There is another change quietly humming away underneath much of our cultural confusion, and it rarely makes the front page because it sounds a bit old-fashioned: the slow decline of the kind of education that once taught people how to think.

For a long time, the backbone of education in liberal democracies wasn't just training people to get jobs. It was training them to reason, to argue and to disagree without immediately losing their minds. Students were introduced to the long, messy conversation that began with the Greeks – Plato asking what justice meant, Aristotle trying to work out what a good life actually looked like – then carried through to Roman law, the Renaissance and the Enlightenment, before eventually shaping the political ideas that underpin modern democratic societies.

You didn't have to agree with any of it. In fact, half the point was that you wouldn't. The exercise was learning how to wrestle with ideas that were bigger than you. You read arguments, you picked them apart, you defended your own position and occasionally realised you might be wrong. It was intellectual sparring – a bit like going to the gym, but for the brain. Somewhere in the last thirty years, that habit has started to fade.

Education has gradually shifted from forming citizens to producing workers. Schools talk about competencies, outcomes and pathways. Universities advertise employability statistics and graduate outcomes. The question quietly changed from 'what should an educated person understand about the world?' to 'what skills does the labour market need this quarter?'

At the same time, the cultural extremes discovered that education is a very effective place to fight their battles. If you want to shape the future, start by shaping the curriculum. So classrooms that once revolved around debating ideas increasingly became places where certain conclusions are quietly assumed before the discussion even begins.

On one side, you find ideological certainty wrapped in moral righteousness. On the other, you find reactionary attempts to drag the curriculum backwards to some imagined golden age. Neither side seems particularly interested in teaching students how to think. They are far more interested in teaching them what to think.

Into that gap marched a new kind of entrepreneur of argument. Charlie Kirk was one of them. He died the way he had lived, shot on a university stage while doing what had made him famous: turning campus politics into a travelling culture-war roadshow. Whatever you thought of his politics, on campuses that had become safe hothouses for one flavour of certainty, he and people like him forced open arguments that had been quietly shut down - and watching the political left celebrate his murder as karmic justice was its own little moral stress test, which a lot of allegedly compassionate people failed. You can spend years arguing that someone's ideas are reckless and still refuse to clap when their heart stops.

Layered over all of this is another social shift: the rise of helicopter parenting. For generations, children were expected to negotiate the world with a certain degree of independence. They got things wrong, they argued with teachers, they occasionally failed exams and lived to tell the tale. The classroom was a place where students were expected to wrestle with difficult ideas, uncomfortable feedback and the occasional bruised ego.

Today, many schools operate under a different pressure. Parents hover. Emails arrive within minutes of a disappointing mark. Teachers find themselves negotiating not only with students but with parents who treat every piece of feedback like a customer complaint. The child's self-esteem becomes a delicate museum artefact that must never be exposed to criticism. The predictable result is that intellectual discomfort, which is precisely what produces learning, increasingly gets treated like a service failure.

Students absorb the lesson quickly. If disagreement feels unpleasant, escalate. If criticism appears, appeal. If a grade disappoints, challenge the process. Teachers, meanwhile, quietly learn that pushing students too hard generates complaints, meetings and paperwork. So the curriculum softens, the standards drift and the difficult conversations that once sharpened minds gradually disappear.

None of this happened because someone woke up and decided civilisation would be improved by making people less thoughtful and more like dumb cunts. Systems simply drift. Governments want measurable outcomes. Universities want enrolments. Activists want influence. Parents want reassurance. Administrators want fewer complaints.

The result is an education system that has become very good at delivering credentials and increasingly patchy at delivering intellectual backbone. Universities now hand out degrees the way airlines hand out boarding passes – efficiently, professionally and with no real guarantee that anyone understands where they're actually going.

At the same time, the cost of the ticket keeps climbing. Students graduate carrying debts that would have startled their parents' generation, only to enter a labour market where starting salaries often look suspiciously similar to what earlier graduates earned decades ago. The price of the credential rises steadily while the economic return becomes less certain. None of this means education has lost its value. Quite the opposite. But it does raise an uncomfortable question: if the cost of degrees keeps soaring while intellectual standards drift and wages stagnate, what exactly are students paying for?

The outcome is not a generation of idiots. Far from it. Young people today can master technology, absorb information and multitask in ways that would have looked like wizardry thirty years ago. What many of them were never properly taught is how to follow an argument all the way to the end, weigh competing ideas without immediately sorting people into good and evil, or disagree without assuming the other person must be stupid or malicious.

Take that habit away and something else moves in. Volume replaces reasoning. Identity replaces argument. Anger replaces persuasion. And while everyone is busy yelling at each other across the barricades, the quiet people in the ordinary rooms keep moving the numbers around.

Which, as it happens, suits the cunts in the shadows just fine.

8

AFTER THE CENTRE – INSTITUTIONS, MEDIA AND THE WIDENING GAP

When the mixed-economy centre was relatively strong, the worst impulses on both sides were at least partly constrained. Regulators sometimes did their jobs. Media outlets sometimes shamed blatant excess. Political parties that actually stood for something depended on outright majorities or broad coalitions, which made it harder to wander too far from the middle without losing elections. The social contract – the quiet agreement not to treat other people as expendable – still had enough living believers to matter.

WHEN THE CENTRE THINS OUT

Trade unions, for all their flaws – and they have many – could push back when employers or governments pushed their luck. They were rarely polite about it, but that was the point: they reminded everyone that "efficiency" and "shareholder value" were not, in fact, higher powers.

Underneath the strikes, the speeches and the badly photocopied leaflets was something quieter and more important – a place where people who did boring jobs for mediocre pay could feel that their voice actually counted for something.

In recent years, though, some unions have started to look less like broad churches for workers and more like small, highly motivated political parties or, in a few depressing cases, convenient vehicles for criminal outfits looking for leverage and cashflow. Parts of the movement now sound as if they've marched several notches further left, more interested in permanent ideological combat than in the grubby, necessary business of haggling over pay, hours and conditions.

Churches, clubs, migrant associations and the occasional local busybody formed the informal guardrails of civic life, constantly reminding people that they lived among neighbours, not just among demographics, market segments or ideological tribes. You went to mass on a Sunday, or the football club on a Saturday, or the Wednesday night committee meeting, and whether you liked it or not you had to sit through other people's opinions, dramas and fundraising raffles. In return, you got casseroles when someone died, a couch to sleep on when things went bad, and the faint but vital sense that you belonged to a "we" larger than whatever was in your bank account.

These institutions were messy, argumentative and often hypocritical. The union delegate could be a pain in the arse, the priest could be pompous, the club president could be drunk with the power of controlling the key to the storeroom. But they performed a simple and important function: they forced people who disagreed with each other to keep sharing the same rooms. They turned strangers into colleagues, parishioners, teammates, comrades – anything other than abstract enemies on a comment thread.

That is the unglamorous magic of institutions: they give people a role, a place to show up, a reason to be counted. You might join for the cheap beer or the chance to get your roster changed, but you stay because somewhere along the way it starts to matter that you're the treasurer, the shop steward, the person who always brings the cake. Purpose doesn't just descend from the heavens; it gets built out of these small, repetitive acts of turning up.

At its best, that centre said, "We will let markets work where they are good at allocating resources, but we will tax, regulate and spend so that the benefits do not pool entirely at the top. We will tolerate wealth but not feudalism. We will allow ambition but try to set a floor beneath so people do not fall." Just as importantly, the "we" in that sentence included people who did not look like you, pray like you or speak your first language.

Over recent decades, that centre has thinned out. Political parties that once represented mass memberships have become hollow marketing machines. Unions have weakened or descended into criminality. Local civic institutions have withered. Churches and other places of faith, where people once sat through often laborious sermons in exchange for a shared story about who they were to each other – and the feeling that they were serving something higher than their own appetites – have emptied out or turned into lifestyle brands with better lighting.

Many people know more about neighbours' online opinions than neighbours' names on their street. People have been trained to see themselves as brands and consumers first, citizens a distant second. If something goes wrong, you are encouraged to ask not "what have we built?" but "what am I feeling?" Feelings become the main currency, and the easiest feelings to manufacture in bulk are fear and resentment.

The problem is not that feelings are bad, but that they are light: they shift by the hour, can be faked on command and bought at scale. As the centre has thinned out, so has our sense of purpose; we are slowly forgetting what it feels like to live for something bigger than ourselves.

Into that vacuum stride the utopian cunts with their simpler stories and sharper elbows. On parts of the left, the focus shifts from building durable economic arrangements to endless moral emergencies. Capitalism itself is declared irredeemable, compromise a sell-out, and anyone who worries about what happens after the barricades is accused of cowardice or complicity. On parts of the right, every argument about tax, welfare, housing or crime is flattened into a culture war about "real" Australians, "real" patriots, traditional values and the supposed threat posed by minorities, migrants and anyone who will not stay in their assigned place.

In both cases, the dull arithmetic of who actually owns what, who gets what share and who is one pay cheque away from disaster gets buried under slogans. "The workers" and "the people" become mascots for arguments they never wrote. The quieter reality – that many of the people screaming past each other online are equally broke and equally anxious – is bad for ratings and fundraising. Far easier to tell a white warehouse worker that their enemy is a brown Uber driver, or to tell a struggling student that their real problem is the existence of boomers, rather than follow the money up the ladder.

THE LONELY MIDDLE

The combined effect of all this is not just material stress but a particular kind of loneliness. You can live in a city of millions, scroll past hundreds of faces a day and still feel like nobody would notice if you quietly vanished. The clubs, unions, congregations and committees that once forced people into the same rooms have thinned out, and in their place we have feeds, comment sections and the occasional algorithmically-assigned "community" that dissolves the minute you log off.

Trust frays in that environment. If your experience of institutions is forms, hold music and scandals, and your experience of other people is drive-by outrage and curated perfection, it gets harder to believe that anyone is really on your side. You may not be able to articulate it in a survey, but your nervous system gets the message: don't rely on anyone, don't stick your neck out, assume there is a catch.

Loneliness like that is not just a sad feeling; it is a political condition. People who feel disconnected and disposable are easier to scare, easier to flatter and easier to recruit. A conspiracy theory or a culture-war crusade offers something the real world no longer reliably does: a story that makes sense of your anger and a group that tells you you're right to feel it. It is no coincidence that some of the loudest online warriors are also some of the most isolated offline.

THE MEDIA, THE FEED AND THE VANISHING CENTRE

It used to be simple. A handful of newspapers, a few TV bulletins, some radio, and that was your window on the world. The mainstream press decided what mattered, in what order, and in what tone. They were biased, smug and occasionally corrupt, but they at least kept up the pretence that their job was to tell you what was going on. There was such a thing as the front page or the six-o'clock news, and if something made it there, it felt real.

Then the internet took a sledgehammer to the gates. Anyone with a phone could publish, broadcast and amplify. The barrier between "audience" and "media" collapsed into a comment thread. Information stopped arriving in edited bundles and started pouring out as an endless stream. Instead of three channels, you got three hundred tabs, a dozen apps and a notification every time someone, somewhere, had a feeling. The promise sounded noble: more voices, more perspectives, more democracy. Who needs a newsroom when you have a timeline?

The trouble is that the old system, for all its faults, didn't just curate information; it also absorbed some of the madness. Editors, whatever their prejudices, were paid to ask "Is this true?" before slapping something on the front page. Once attention became the main currency, that question quietly changed. The key test stopped being "Is it true?" and became "Will it engage?" Truth is slow, conditional and often boring. Engagement is fast, emotional and instantly measurable. Guess which one wins in a meeting about quarterly targets.

Mainstream outlets adapted, just not in the direction of monk-like integrity. They learned to chase clicks, juice outrage and treat every story as an episode in a never-ending culture war. Headlines became bait. Nuance became a liability. Panels filled with people chosen not because they knew anything useful, but because they could be relied on to generate a clip that 'goes off' online. The old pose of seeker of truth remained for branding purposes, but under the hood the machinery was being rewired for something closer to mood management and audience herding.

At the same time, the individual reader was told this was liberation. You can 'do your own research', pick your own sources, curate your own feed. In theory, that's empowering. In practice, most people do not have the time, training or inclination to sift through mountains of conflicting claims with forensic care. So we do what humans have always done: we look for cues. Who sounds like our tribe? Who flatters what we already believe? Who makes us feel justified instead of uncertain? The result is not a great marketplace of ideas, but a set of parallel universes, each with its own facts, villains and preferred apocalypse.

The new media environment excels at one thing above all: manipulation, not in the cartoon sense of a man stroking a cat in a bunker, but in the banal way built into the business model. If your revenue depends on people staying engaged, your content will slide, inch by inch, toward whatever keeps them scrolling. Fear keeps people scrolling. So does outrage, humiliation, envy and the thrill of watching some poor bastard "destroyed" in thirty seconds. The recommendation systems learn this faster than any human editor, and quietly reshape the information diet accordingly.

Mainstream outlets, terrified of irrelevance, plug themselves into the same circuitry. Stories are chosen because they will travel. Angles are tweaked for maximum reaction. Entire news cycles are reverse-engineered from whatever is trending, as if a malfunctioning global mood ring had been promoted to editor-in-chief. The old fantasy that the media was a neutral mirror of reality has died; in its place is a hall of mirrors, carefully arranged to maximise attention and, by extension, profit or power.

This doesn't mean good journalism has vanished. There are still reporters risking their necks, fact-checkers combing documents, editors killing stories that don't stand up. They just now operate inside a system that treats their work as one more content stream, to be sliced into viral moments and surrounded by outrage-bait and sponsored nonsense. Truth survives, but often as a side-effect, not the organising purpose. The operating question is no longer "What is happening and how do we explain it?" but "What keeps them here and how do we get them back tomorrow?"

For the individual, the result is a kind of hyper-informed ignorance. You can know, in exquisite detail, what a stranger on the other side of the world thinks about a celebrity divorce, while having only the faintest idea how your local budget works or who actually regulates your rent, your water, your air. You feel constantly "up to date" and yet have no stable picture of reality, because the stream never pauses long enough to let you see the whole river. What you believe becomes less a product of evidence and more a product of where you happen to stand in the attention economy.

And this is where the centre starts to vanish. When most people drank from the same few information wells, they at least argued about the same weather report. You could disagree violently about what it meant, but you were pointing at the same sky. Now two neighbours can open their phones and be told that completely different things are on fire, with each feed screaming that its fire is the only one that matters. The centre – the place where you admit the world is complicated, and other people might have a point – struggles to compete with that kind of bespoke catastrophe.

Emotion beats evidence nine times out of ten in this ecosystem. Calm, qualified takes sink without a trace. Sharp, absolutist, outrage-drenched takes get showered with likes, follows and algorithmic love. Over time, people behave accordingly. If you stick to the moderate middle, your voice disappears. If you edge further out and shout a bit louder, you get rewarded. The architecture doesn't need to tell you what to think; it just tutors you in how to behave if you want to be seen.

The system also makes it easy to live inside caricatures. You see more of what you react to, less of what you ignore. Click on one clip about how "the other side" is insane, and you'll be offered a hundred more. Your mental picture of your opponents gets built out of their noisiest, most ridiculous representatives. After a while, it feels not only unnecessary but positively immoral to compromise with people your feed has rendered as monsters. Why meet in the middle with someone you're now convinced wants to destroy everything you value?

Meanwhile, trust in any common referee evaporates. The old media may have been partial, but they at least gestured at a shared standard of fact. Now every outlet is assumed to be somebody's weapon. If you're on the right, the mainstream is a left-wing plot. If you're on the left, it's a corporate gas-lighting machine. If you're simply exhausted, you decide they're all lying anyway. In that atmosphere, the idea of a shared, evidence-based centre starts to look like a charming superstition from a more innocent age.

So the change is not just that we have more information. We have built an information environment that is superb at producing certainty without knowledge, emotion without context and identity without community. It pulls us away from the messy, half-satisfying work of the centre – compromise, patience, the slow testing of claims against reality – and towards corners where we can feel pure, angry and absolutely right. It is very good at making us fans, enemies and addicts. It is much less interested in helping us remain citizens.

THE WIDENING GAP

As the centre erodes, the gap between rich and poor yawns open even in countries that like to lecture others about fairness, democracy and human rights. At the top end of the ladder, wealth begins to behave less like income and more like gravity. Once you have enough of it, more arrives almost automatically. Assets appreciate while their owners are on holiday. Investments compound while their owners are asleep. Capital gains quietly outpace wages. Tax structures smooth the path. Entire industries emerge whose sole purpose is to keep the upward flow moving politely and efficiently.

At the other end of the spectrum, life moves in the opposite direction. The bottom slices of society rotate between insecure jobs, stagnant wages and debts that never quite shrink. Rent climbs faster than income.

Energy bills creep upward. Healthcare, childcare and education quietly become luxuries disguised as services. A broken car, a sick child or a rent increase can unravel months of careful budgeting in a single week.

Growing up, the charity ads on television usually showed a dusty road somewhere in Africa and a solemn voice asking you to sponsor a child for less than a dollar a day. The message was clear: poverty was something tragic that happened far away, in countries with weak institutions and fragile economies.

These days, the appeals look different. Increasingly, they feature Australian children whose families cannot afford the basic necessities for school uniforms, lunches, textbooks and transport. The geography of hardship has shifted uncomfortably closer to home. The numbers tell the same story. Estimates suggest that well over a million Australians live on or below the poverty line, including hundreds of thousands of children.

In a country that still likes to describe itself as one of the most prosperous societies on earth, that is not a statistical curiosity. It is a warning light. The numbers alone are stark enough. But the deeper shift is psychological.

Between the rich and the struggling sits the middle, the people who were told for decades that they were the backbone of the system. Teachers. Nurses. Electricians. Office workers. Small business owners. Public servants. For a long time, they believed in a fairly simple bargain: work hard, follow the rules, pay your taxes, contribute to society and eventually you would achieve some stability. That meant:

- a home that did not feel like a speculative asset
- a job that did not disappear every election cycle
- a future that moved forward, even if slowly.

The bargain was never perfect, but it was real enough to anchor millions of lives. Now it is starting to wobble. Increasingly, the middle finds itself one redundancy, one illness or one interest rate rise away from joining the people it was trained to look down on. The mortgage that once symbolised arrival now feels more like a countdown clock. The safety nets that once caught falling families have quietly frayed.

You can see the anxiety everywhere. Parents running spreadsheets late at night trying to work out whether their children will ever afford a home. Professionals quietly calculating how long their savings would last if the job disappeared. Young adults watching property prices rise faster than their careers and wondering whether the ladder has simply been pulled up behind them.

The public story, however, remains carefully curated. If you are idle, reckless or criminal, you deserve what you get. If you are struggling despite doing everything right, the system is regrettable but unchangeable. And if you are doing extraordinarily well, you earned it. Full stop.

Meanwhile, the machinery that quietly shifts wealth upward rarely makes the front page. Tax systems that favour capital over labour. Privatisation deals that transfer public assets into private hands. Wage growth that lags behind productivity. The slow starving of public services until their decline becomes the justification for selling them. These are described as technical adjustments, fiscal discipline, market efficiency.

Question them and you are accused of envy, ignorance or class warfare. At the same time, the mechanisms that funnel suspicion downward are broadcast loudly and constantly. Dog-whistling about crime and borders. Hysteria about invasions. Jokes about no-go zones. Every economic anxiety is gently redirected towards a human scapegoat.

No grand conspiracy is required. Large systems simply have a tendency to grow and justify their own existence. The result is an odd imbalance: the people taking risks in the real economy spend increasing amounts of time navigating forms and approvals, while the institutions managing those systems become larger, safer and more permanent.

9

CUNTS WHO LIVE IN THE SHADOWS

When the gap between rich and poor widens, something else widens with it: the distance between ordinary people and the decisions that shape their lives. In healthy societies, power feels visible. You may not like the government, the bank, the council or the regulator, but you roughly understand who is responsible and how decisions get made. When the middle begins to wobble and the ground beneath people's lives feels less stable, that clarity starts to dissolve.

Decisions appear to come from somewhere else, from rooms no one voted for, from rules nobody remembers approving, from institutions that seem to outlast every election. That is when people start asking a simple question: who the hell is actually running this place? And when power becomes hard to see, it does not disappear. It simply retreats into the shadows, into committees, boardrooms, advisory panels and late-night amendments where decisions can be made quietly and responsibility spreads thin enough that nobody seems to own it.

THE BEIGE OFFICE

If you want to picture the cunts who live in the shadows, forget movie villains stroking cats in underground lairs. Think instead of very boring people in very ordinary offices, moving numbers between columns and paragraphs between pages. Think of the person who writes the regulation that decides whether your building needs sprinklers, the banker who decides whether your developer gets a loan, the politician who nods through a planning change at 10:37 pm in a half-empty chamber. Nobody chants their name. Nobody prints them on a T-shirt. But your life bends around their choices.

The disharmony is not an accident. It is insulation. It is a fog machine on full blast so the rest of us cannot see who is actually wiring the building. The more time we spend calling each other traitors, snowflakes, boomers, freeloaders, class enemies or sheeple, the less time and energy we have left for dull questions about who wrote this law, who paid for that campaign and why a contract went to that mate on that day.

Every conspiracy theory starts with a hunch that you are being played. Someone, somewhere, is pulling the strings. Conspiracists talk about a deep state. Activists talk about dark money. Your uncle on Facebook talks about globalist cabals, reptilian overlords and tracking chips in vaccines. Most of it is, technically speaking, horseshit. There is no single control room where one bloke in a cloak pulls all the levers. There is no master spreadsheet labelled 'How we will ruin Dave from unit 703'.

But the conspiracy nuts are not wrong about the feeling. They are just crap at the diagnosis. They know, at gut level, that power has gone somewhere they cannot see. They know decisions that shape their lives are being made in rooms they will never enter, in conversations they will never hear, using language designed to make normal people feel stupid for even asking. They cannot see the wiring, so they invent a cartoon, secret cabals, omnipotent elites, magic documents that explain everything.

The cartoon is wrong in the details and dangerous in the consequences. But the itch it scratches is real. The real wiring is not the alien lizards, Satanic pizza shops or all-seeing eye on the back of the dollar. It's the very human, very fallible, very entitled networks of people who quietly thrive when the centre falls apart and the rest of us are too busy shouting at the stage to notice who owns the theatre.

DEEP STATE, SHALLOW TRUTHS

Let us start with the phrase that launched a thousand YouTube channels – the deep state.

In the Trumpian version, the deep state is a shadow government of unelected officials and security spooks who spend their days plotting how to frustrate the noble will of one orange man and his chosen people. In other versions, it is permanent bureaucrats, judges, generals, intelligence chiefs – anyone who outlasts a four-year electoral cycle and occasionally says no to a leader who is convinced that democracy means 'I get what I want'.

There is a grain of truth there. Modern states do have layers you cannot vote out in one go. There are senior public servants, central bankers, police commissioners, surveillance agencies and regulators, all with powers that matter to your life and are not up for election every three years. There are also the corporate and financial actors who move faster than any parliament, major banks, insurers, tech platforms, fossil fuel companies and logistics giants. They are not underground. They are just not answerable to you.

So yes, there is a deep part of the state and the economy, deep in the sense that it sits under and around party politics, deep in the sense that it does not flip every time a few suburbs change their vote. Where the fairytale goes off the rails is when it turns that messy ecosystem into a single, conscious villain. It takes a very complicated, very human web of institutions and incentives and flattens it into a Marvel movie, one Supreme Council of Bastards, stroking their white cats and assigning each other regions.

Why does that story sell? Because it is satisfying. A single villain can be slain. A single secret can be revealed. It is much harder to get people fired up about the slow grind of reforming planning law, or rewriting conflict of interest rules, or tightening disclosure obligations for campaign donors. For the people actually sitting in those deep layers, the conspiracy stuff is a mixed blessing. On Mondays, it is annoying. They see Joe in Accounts being accused of rigging global energy prices when Joe's main crime is sending passive-aggressive emails about timesheets. On Tuesdays, it is extremely useful. As long as their critics look like lunatics, they can wave away any legitimate questions as more of the same. 'Oh, you want to know why I met that lobbyist three times last month? What are you, one of those deep state nuts?'

The cartoon deep state and the real, boring deep state have a symbiotic relationship. One feeds the other. One makes people angry enough to distrust everything, the other relies on that exhaustion to keep operating with minimal scrutiny. It is a beautiful racket, if you are into that sort of thing.

HOW DISHARMONY BECOMES A BUSINESS MODEL

When politics was anchored, however imperfectly, in a chunky centre, the loudest utopians on both sides were kept somewhat in check. They could yell, they could run, they could even occasionally win office, but they had to deal with institutions, unions, churches, parties with mass memberships and independent media that dragged them back towards compromise. As that centre thinned out, something else took its place: permanent campaign mode.

Winning the next outrage cycle became more important than running the country, or the state, or the city, like a shared home. Every issue could be turned into an identity test. Are you with the good people or the scum? Nuance became treason. That is a nightmare if you are trying to pass complex, boring legislation in public. It is a dream if you are a cunt in the shadows.

Hyperpolarised politics turns citizens into superfans. Once you are a fan, you will forgive your team for almost anything short of eating a puppy on live television, and even then you will demand to see the full context. Did it bark at them first? Were there jobs at stake?

While you are busy defending the jersey, the people in the shadows are signing away your bargaining power at work, your right to contest planning decisions, your future tax base and your kids' school funding. You get a culture war victory. They get the keys to the safe.

Here is how the business model works:

- **Step One:** Keep everybody emotionally jacked up. Rage, fear, disgust, righteousness – anything but calm curiosity. Calm people ask awkward questions and read documents. Angry people share memes and join mobs.

- **Step Two:** Make sure every boring decision is framed as a side effect, not a choice. A tax cut that overwhelmingly favours asset owners – that is boosting investment. A planning change that lets developers pack more floors into already strained suburbs – that is cutting red tape. A wage-suppression policy – that is maintaining competitiveness. None of these are presented as taking X from group A and giving it to group B, even though that is exactly what they do.

- **Step Three:** When someone notices the pattern and complains, give them a villain that is not you. Blame the elites in general, or woke corporations, or lazy welfare bludgers, or foreigners. Sell them a story about moral decay, cultural invasion, weak leadership – anything that directs their anger sideways instead of upwards.

The more the public argues about drag queens and Australia Day and flags and slogans, the more leeway there is behind the scenes to do what you were going to do anyway. The more we fight about who kneels during the anthem, the less we notice who owns the stadium. The everyday deep state, your parliament, your town hall. All of this sounds big and far away until you realise you have already met these people. You just call them different names.

THE DEEP STATE

In politics, the deep state is not a secret cabal in cloaks. It is a recurring set of names on press releases, donor lists and committee minutes. It is the junior minister who is somehow always on the taskforce that recommends what their favourite lobby group already wanted. It is the staffer who just drafts the talking points but mysteriously writes them in a way that protects the same sponsors every time. It is the backroom fixer who never runs for office, never fronts a camera, but always seems to be in the room when deals are done.

It is the pollster who explains, with a weary smile, that there is no appetite for housing reform or treaty or proper corruption watchdogs, because their focus group of twelve people in a motel conference room looked uncomfortable. It is the think tank that publishes independent reports which, by sheer coincidence, all recommend policies that benefit the same handful of industries. None of these people are twirling moustaches. Most would describe themselves as professionals, even patriots. They are just used to being the ones who get the briefings, used to being deferred to, used to everyone else nodding along because that is how politics works.

If you want to understand the deep state, do not start in Washington. Start in your own parliament or council chamber. Watch who stands at the back of the room during question time, hands in pockets, talking quietly while the cameras point the other way. Watch who the minister greets by first name when they step off the stage.

Watch which backbencher always asks the friendly question written in the same office that wrote the press release. Watch which journalists get the leaks and which ones get frozen out.

Now add division.

If the public is already at war with itself, city against regions, young against old, renters against owners, battlers against dole bludgers, the shadow cluster has maximum freedom. Nobody can form a stable majority around boring, grown-up reforms like campaign finance laws or independent anti-corruption bodies, because they are too busy trying to crush the people they see as enemies. Half the country would rather set its own hair on fire than vote for any policy attached to That Party They Hate.

From the shadows, this is ideal. You only need a small, disciplined group to steer decisions if everyone else is fragmented, furious and tired. You do not even have to rig the vote. You just have to keep turning up, keep returning calls, keep donating on time, keep feeding the right outrage stories to the right outlets, and let the noise work in your favour.

CONSPIRACY THEORIES AS SEDATIVES AND ACCELERANTS

When people finally notice that things they never agreed to are happening – water privatised, surveillance powers expanded, public land flogged off, resource rent tax not collected – they reach for the stories they have at hand. In this decade, those stories are rarely 'maybe we should examine the governance structure and incentive alignment in this institution'. They are far more likely to be 'they are all in on it'.

In politics, that might sound like the following:

- 'All politicians are corrupt.'
- 'The media and the government are working together to control us.'
- 'This has all been planned from the start.'

Sometimes there is a grain of truth. Yes, people skim. Yes, people collude. Yes, people lie. Often, though, what is really going on is more banal and more depressing: incompetence, laziness, favouritism, tribal loyalty, fear of losing the next election. Nobody had to mastermind a plot to underfund mental health for twenty years. They just had to keep choosing short-term savings and photo ops over long-term responsibility.

Conspiracy thinking does two unhelpful things at once: it overpersonalises everything, and it discredits legitimate critique. The first keeps you in a permanent state of hypervigilance, fear and rage - exhausted people make terrible citizens, they either lash out at random targets or give up altogether. The second makes it easy to dismiss anyone raising genuine concerns about lobbying, regulatory capture or cosy tender processes, because the loudest voices questioning power are busy raving about microchips in vaccines and paedophile rings in pizza shops.

This is the genius of modern cunthood in the shadows. You do not have to silence your critics. You just have to make sure the loudest ones are ridiculous. As long as the opposition to your power comes dressed in capes, yelling about chemtrails, you can keep signing the contracts. When someone sensible asks why multinational gas companies are able to extract our natural gas for cents on the dollar, you shrug and point at the bloke on a YouTube channel explaining how the earth is flat and run by vegans. 'See, conspiracy nuts. Nothing to worry about.'

The dynamic in politics is bigger than a building, but the pattern is exactly the same. The one journalist, whistleblower or backbencher who notices patterns and asks hard questions gets lumped in with the chronic ranter who rings talkback every night with theories about secret armies under the supermarket. 'They are all crazy.'

Easier to ignore them both than to separate the person who needs medication from the person who has noticed that the same donors, and the same expert panels keep turning up whenever public money is on the table.

ENTITLEMENT, COWARDICE AND CRUELTY IN ORDINARY ROOMS

The three pillars mentioned earlier – entitlement, cowardice, cruelty – do not disappear in the shadows. They just put on a blazer.

Entitlement in this world sounds reasonable:

- 'I have been here a long time.'
- 'I understand the bigger picture.'
- 'These decisions are complex; the average person would not get it.'

It is the policy adviser who thinks public consultation is a box-ticking exercise because the minister already has a direction. It is the chair who edits minutes to make sure nothing awkward is on the record. It is the manager who rolls their eyes when owners ask to see invoices. Underneath is a simple belief: my judgement is worth more than your consent.

Cowardice presents as process. 'We followed the correct procedures.' 'Independent advice was sought.' 'The market has spoken.' Nobody decided to price poor people out of safe housing; that was just how the numbers stacked up. Nobody chose to leave an obviously dangerous building standing; that was a matter for the regulator. Nobody chose to ignore whistleblowers; that was an HR issue. Responsibility dissolves into forms, workflows, committees, external consultants. The line demanded it. The spreadsheet insisted.

Cruelty does not shout. It does not have to. It signs. It delays. It notes and defers and acknowledges concerns while quietly doing nothing. It lets mould spread because fixing it would blow the maintenance budget this quarter. It lets cladding stay on because removing it would spook the market. It lets a toxic manager stay in place because sacking them would mean admitting a mistake.

Shadow cunthood is not less cunty. It is just less noisy. You do not get gulags. You get decades of avoidable misery, scattered across thousands of lives in doses just small enough that nobody declares a national emergency. Instead of one big atrocity, you get a thousand small, plausible-sounding decisions that add up, if you zoom out, to a very clear message: your comfort is optional, our convenience is not.

ELITES, EPSTEIN AND THE MYTH OF SUPERIORITY

Sitting comfortably above the widening gap is a class that barely bothers to hide itself anymore. For years we have heard stories about shadowy global elites pulling the strings, puppetmasters hovering above governments, markets and media. Most of those stories are cartoonish. But every now and then reality tears a small hole in the curtain and you see something uglier behind it. The Epstein files were one of those moments.

Millions of pages of court records, flight logs, calendars, photographs and correspondence tied a convicted sex offender and alleged trafficker into a network of the rich and powerful - presidents, princes, CEOs, academics, lawyers, media figures. The documents do not prove that every name mentioned committed crimes. Even the filings make that clear. What they do prove is proximity, access and a shared assumption that this man belonged comfortably inside the inner ring of power.

And if those files taught us anything, it is this: there is nothing elite about the elites at all. You are not elite if your idea of power involves flying vulnerable little girls to private islands for the amusement of rich men and women. You are not elite if your status depends on hurting the weakest people you can find. You are not elite if your fantasies revolve around domination, humiliation and the kind of cruelty that requires lawyers, pilots and security staff to keep it running smoothly. That does not make you a mastermind. It makes you a cunt. A particularly depraved one, but still just a cunt.

The so-called global elites who orbited Epstein's world were not puppetmasters operating on some higher plane of intelligence. They were the same old human pattern on a more expensive carpet: the entitlement of men and women who assumed status made them untouchable, the cowardice of institutions that chose not to look too closely, and the cruelty of complete indifference to the people at the bottom of those arrangements - the bodies that made the parties and the favours possible.

The Epstein world was not an alien conspiracy. It was simply what happens when ordinary, flawed human beings are handed extraordinary wealth, insulation and flattery, and then told, subtly or otherwise, that the rules no longer apply to them.

The conspiracy theorists get one thing half right: there really are circles where money and status loosen the rules. Doors open more easily. Police become more cautious. Scandals are managed rather than punished. You do not end up on those guest lists because you are a humble servant of the common good. But the conspiracists also give these people far too much credit.

They are not super-geniuses orchestrating the planet from a secret command centre. They are not gods. They are toddlers with nuclear codes and black Amex cards – humans with appetites, vanity and too few guardrails. The wiring that protects them is the same wiring that protects the smaller, more boring shadow cunts in planning departments, procurement panels and ministerial offices. The scale is different. The pattern is identical.

Our real mistake has been to accept the branding. We call these people philanthropists, global leaders, innovators. We treat charity galas and keynote speeches as evidence of character rather than clever public relations. Every time we use the word *elite* without irony, we accidentally flatter them, reinforcing the illusion that they operate on a higher moral plane. The Epstein files should have killed that illusion stone dead.

What they revealed was not a secret order of masterminds. They revealed that some of the people elbowing their way to the top of decision-making chains are profoundly unimpressive human beings who happened to accumulate enormous power and protection. Individuals capable of trading a child's suffering for a weekend's entertainment and then returning home to deliver speeches about leadership, responsibility and family values.

So when we talk about cunts in the shadows, do not just picture the mid-level fixer quietly editing a regulation at 10:37 pm. Picture the private island. The guest list. The pilots, lawyers, security staff and assistants. The politicians and CEOs who concluded this was normal, or at least not worth asking too many questions about.

Picture the entire ecosystem required to keep a monster comfortable and the story quiet. And notice something important. The way you stop that kind of horror is not by inventing bigger conspiracy theories on Facebook. It is by dragging as much of the wiring as possible into daylight. It is by refusing to treat wealth, fame or office as proof of virtue. It is by building institutions that do not care how many private jets you own when the accusation lands.

If the word *elite* is going to mean anything worth keeping, it should mean the opposite of untouchable. It should mean more accountable, not less, because the consequences of your decisions travel further. The people desperate to sit near power do not magically transform into guardians of the common good once they arrive. The Epstein files were a reminder of something simpler and older: a culture that confuses status with character is begging to be exploited.

And a society that keeps bowing politely to its so-called elites should not be surprised when some of them turn out to be just another species of cunt – only richer, quieter, and protected by better lawyers.

DRAGGING THE WIRING INTO THE DAYLIGHT

If this were just a book about how everyone is awful and everything is rigged, it would end here, with a drink and a nervous laugh. 'We are all fucked. Cheers.' But that is not the point. The point is to see clearly enough that you can start behaving differently without lying to yourself about the scale of the problem. The cunts in the shadows rely on your boredom, your exhaustion and your appetite for simple stories. Take away any two of those and they start to sweat.

This does not mean you need to become a full-time activist or a professional pain in the arse. It means, at minimum, when something big is at stake – your home, your workplace, your city – you read the paper before you sign. Not the glossy summary, but the actual terms. You pay attention to who benefits and who pays. You follow the money, the approvals, the appointments. If the same names keep showing up in the benefits column, that is not an accident.

You do not let your ideological team jersey stop you from seeing when your side is doing exactly what you would call out as corruption or cowardice if the other side did it. You stop treating the word 'elite' as a compliment and start treating it as a warning label – handle with suspicion.

At the political level, it might mean voting for people who occasionally tell you something you do not want to hear. Supporting reforms that limit donations, closing revolving doors and publishing more information as default, even when those reforms irritate your tribe. Choosing media that shows you uncomfortable facts, not just dopamine hits of outrage that flatter your existing views.

None of this is sexy. That is the point. The centre died partly because we got bored with it. The cunts in the shadows multiplied because we left them alone with the wiring while we went looking for more stimulating enemies. But it's not about finding a mythical leader who will storm the hidden bunker and free us from the deep state. It's about learning how to live and act in full knowledge that there are cunts in the shadows, and then refusing to hand them any more power than they already stole.

You cannot shut them down completely. You can make their job harder. You can shrink the gaps they slip through. You can rebuild a centre that is thick enough, nosy enough and grown-up enough that they can no longer treat the rest of us as background noise. That starts, unglamorously, with this decision: to stop being a spectator in someone else's puppet show and start tugging on a few strings yourself, even if it means sitting through the dullest meeting in the world, and being the only one in the room who still remembers what the words 'shared responsibility' were supposed to mean.

10

HOW NOT TO BE A CUNT, ON PURPOSE

The natural response is to step back, wash your hands of the lot and declare yourself above it all and move to an off grid cabin in the woods. 'They're all corrupt. They're all clowns. I'll look after me and mine, vote when I have to, and otherwise treat politics and committees like the weather: annoying, but not my fault.'

That is exactly how cunthood wins.

It almost never wins with a single dramatic coup. It wins through drift. It wins because, while decent people are sighing and switching off, the most entitled, cowardly and cruel people in the room are very much switching on. It wins because we let our own worst impulses go unchecked, and because we treat the maintenance of a grown-up centre, in our buildings, workplaces and countries, as somebody else's job.

Entitlement says, 'My comfort first.' Cowardice says, 'My skin first.' Cruelty says, 'My side first.' Put them together and you get a person who will happily sacrifice the common good as long as their own small world stays warm and undisturbed. The alternative is not sainthood. The alternative is an adult centre, people who are willing, in small and large ways, to sacrifice comfort, reputation and sometimes safety so that something shared can survive. People who know that if nobody is willing to lose a bit on principle, everybody eventually loses a lot on someone else's terms.

But this is not about following the Ten Commandments of Virtue. I am not founding the Church of Not Being a Cunt. This is about the most modest revolution available, becoming just self-aware enough, and just bloody-minded enough, that you;

1. stop sliding into cunthood by default

2. start carrying some of the weight of the centre instead of kicking holes in it for sport.

You are not being asked to be pure. You are being asked to be slightly less of a walking hazard than the average talkback caller. That's it. That's the bar.

THE UTOPIAN IN THE MIRROR

The first obstacle is in the mirror, and it's wearing your face. You have, whether you admit it or not, a little utopian cunt inside you. So do I. It is the part of you that looks at the mess of the world and thinks, 'If people just did what I do, this would all be fine.'

If you're temperamentally leftish, your inner utopian cunt whispers that if we just taxed wealth properly, smashed the oligarchs, cancelled a few reactionaries and gave power to 'the people', equality would fall like summer rain. If you lean rightish, it insists that if we just trusted markets, shot some regulations in the head and stopped mollycoddling idiots with safety nets, prosperity would drift down from the top like champagne bubbles from the penthouse.

If you're into wellness, your utopia probably involves everyone doing yoga and drinking mushroom coffee until it glows. If you're more spiritual than political, the dream looks slightly different: everyone raising their vibration, doing breath work in Bali and speaking from their 'authentic truth' – a truth that, curiously, always requires everyone else to shut up and listen. Different incense, same script.

Your inner utopian tells a simple three-act story:

1. You have been wronged.

2. We have seen the truth.

3. If everyone would just get on board, we could fix this.

It feels righteous. It is also the precise mental space where entitlement, cowardice and cruelty sneak in dressed as virtue.

Because you see the truth, you start to believe you deserve more power than other people. Their doubts become ignorance, your arrogance becomes insight. You stop thinking 'I might be partly wrong' and start thinking 'I am the only sane person in a world of sheeple.' You become too important to be questioned, too enlightened to be inconvenienced, too busy saving the world to stack chairs after the meeting. You can spot this in miniature at any committee. Watch the person who always knows better, never apologises and treats every suggestion as an attack on their destiny. They are not leading; they are rehearsing being a minor dictator in a very small country.

Wrapped in grand words, any harm done in the name of the cause becomes unfortunate but necessary. You didn't scream abuse at that neighbour, you spoke truth to power. You didn't force through that policy that wrecked lives without consultation, you had the courage to act. Responsibility dissolves into history, destiny, revolution, the market - anything but you. You will hear this every time someone says, 'Look, personally I feel bad about it, but that's politics,' while signing something they know is wrong. It is the same move as the middle manager who blames head office, the activist who blames the movement, the landlord who blames how the game works. Everyone is brave right up until there might be a personal cost.

The natural endpoint is cruelty. Once the stakes are high enough in your mind, the people in the way of your preferred future stop being fully human and start being obstacles. They are not mistaken; they are enemies - boomers, wokists, grifters, leeches, Karens. Enemies must be defeated, not persuaded. If a few are crushed along the way, that's progress. It's the little thrill when someone from the other tribe gets dog-piled, fired or dragged through the tabloids. You tell yourself they deserve it. You don't ask whether you would be okay with the same treatment landing on your least favourite cousin.

Your inner utopian is the voice that turns perfectly normal people into petty tyrants on committees, abusive bosses, vindictive landlords, online mobs and politicians who can't look at a chart of harm without immediately asking how it plays with their base. You will not get rid of that voice. The trick is to recognise it early enough that you stop mistaking it for moral clarity. Instead of thinking 'I am finally awake', try 'Ah, there's my brain trying to audition for cult leader again'. That small, embarrassing admission, that you are not immune to bullshit, including your own, is the beginning of sanity.

The people who are safest to trust with power are usually the ones slightly embarrassed to have it. The people who scare you should be the ones who think they were born for the job.

STANDING IN THE BORING MIDDLE

We have been trained to talk about 'the centre' as if it is a political brand. Centrists, moderates, the sensible middle – it sounds like a marketing focus group in human form. No wonder half the population hears 'centre' and thinks 'people who like things exactly as they are, because they're doing fine'.

That is not the centre I'm interested in.

The centre worth defending is not a point on a graph. It is a way of behaving under pressure. It's what happens when adults accept three unpleasant facts at once: that real injustices exist, that fixes are partial and slow, and that we still have to share a society tomorrow.

At the level of a person, the centre is not your knack for finding mushy compromises. The centre is your willingness to pay a cost so that something larger than you does not break. It's the ability to hold two truths in your head without exploding – acknowledging that a situation is unjust and frustrating, while accepting that the practical changes available right now may not deliver everything one hopes for, and still being willing to shoulder a fair share of the responsibility.

It is the opposite of purity. Purity wants policies that express your feelings perfectly. The centre wants outcomes that make things a bit less shit for a lot of people, and is willing to sacrifice comfort, applause and occasionally friendships to get them, without blowing up three other things at the same time.

In the workplace, the centre isn't just nodding along to a neutral policy. It's being the one executive who says, 'No, we're not firing five thousand people weeks after announcing a record profit. We'll cut our own perks first.' And then actually living with the smaller bonus.

It looks like standing in front of a furious staff meeting so the junior manager doesn't have to, and wearing the reputation hit yourself so the work can keep going. It looks like admitting you stuffed up instead of throwing an intern under the bus. It is staying in the boring meeting and reading the boring papers so you can spot the not-boring cruelty buried in the fine print.

In communities, the centre looks like backing social housing on your own street, knowing your property price might take a hit, because other people's kids need a place to sleep before they can worry about capital gains. It looks like chairing the rancid public meeting about disability access and going home shaken and exhausted, but relieved that the ramp passed and the theoretical 'cost to the budget' landed on you instead of the person in the wheelchair.

It may mean walking an elderly neighbour through an online form for the fifth time, even though you are tired and they are slow and nobody is filming it for content. It means taking your turn on the roster instead of letting the same three people run everything until they burn out and move to Tasmania.

In friendship, the centre is not 'being nice'. It looks like having the conversation that might end the friendship because someone's addiction or cruelty is burning down their life and everyone around them. It looks like staying beside them through the fallout, fully aware that some of the social mud will splash onto you.

It is sacrificing your image as the easy friend for the sake of their actual future. Sometimes it's the opposite, quietly stepping back from a relationship that is built on shared spite, on hating the same people, even though it gives you a warm feeling of belonging. The centre knows that solidarity built entirely on mutual loathing eventually turns inwards.

In customer life, the centre is not a five-paragraph review about your feelings. It looks like choosing not to use the tiny power you have over the person on minimum wage to punish them for a bad night. It's absorbing the cold chips and the misspelled name because the world is already hard enough for people with no HR department to hide behind.

It's not demanding to see the manager because your latte arrived at a temperature that wounded your soul. It's tipping the delivery driver even when the app tells you they were 'late', because you can see the rain on their back and the ten-dollar order in their hand.

In politics, the centre looks like voting for a treaty or reform that will cost you friends, followers and some speaking gigs, because you care more about a wounded country than your mentions. It looks like defending due process for people you loathe because you know that once the rules stop applying to them, they can stop applying to anyone.

It looks like resigning from a role rather than carrying out an order that would trash the rule of law, even though nobody will remember your name in thirty years. It might mean backing a dull, competent candidate who reads the brief over a charismatic arsonist who reads the room. It might mean admitting when your own side has stuffed something up and refusing to spin it, even when pointing that out would hand the other side an easy talking point. That last bit is important: the centre behaves as if integrity is not a team sport.

And in your own life, the centre is staying in the room after you lose the vote, not because you enjoy losing, but because you know that storming out, dramatising your own heroism and refusing to engage next time just hands more space to the most committed arseholes in the room. It is carrying more than your share so that something shared can still exist, and doing it knowing there will be no statue, no montage, no 'thank you for your service' beyond maybe an email.

The centre is tedious. It is exhausting. It will rarely make you feel like a legend. Without it, most of the things we like about our lives, from stable currencies to functioning hospitals to buildings that don't fall down, go from 'precarious' to 'fantasy' in about a decade. You do not get a certificate for showing up to the AGM. You just get slightly less chaos next year.

STOP HIDING BEHIND NOUNS

One move that quietly turns decent people into cunts at scale is the habit of outsourcing your conscience to an abstract noun and calling it necessity. You've heard the soundtrack:

- 'The market decided.'
- 'The algorithm flagged them.'
- 'It's just policy.'
- 'These are the rules.'
- 'That's how the system works.'

Sometimes those sentences describe real constraints. There is a law. There is a budget. There is a process. But none of those things arrived in a burning bush. Somebody wrote the law. Somebody set the budget. Somebody designed the process. Somebody decided which variables went into the algorithm and which human beings counted as outliers.

Every time you hide behind one of those nouns to excuse an obviously harmful decision, you take one more step into the guided-missile behaviour we met earlier in the book: harm delivered at a distance, with clean hands and full deniability.

You see it in workplaces that talk about 'headcount optimisation' instead of sacking people. In governments that talk about 'border integrity' instead of desperate families in tents. In tech companies that talk about 'engagement' instead of addiction.

Imagine, instead, that every such decision came with a plaque:

- 'This motion to evict the pensioner in 5B for falling behind on levies was moved by [your name here].'
- 'This decision to award the fire safety contract to a mate's firm without competitive tender and quotes was approved by [your name here].'
- 'This restructuring plan that replaced full-time jobs with unpaid internships was championed by [your name here], who called it 'a great opportunity for young people'.
- 'This 'cost-saving measure' that swapped real fruit for flavoured syrup in the hospital meals came from [your name here], who said it wouldn't affect patient outcomes'.

If you would not be comfortable seeing your name there in black and white, you do not get to comfort yourself with 'the system'. The system is just the wiring. You chose to plug yourself in.

Being less of a cunt does not mean you become a heroic whistleblower every week or set yourself on fire in protest. It might mean something much less cinematic and much more demanding, like quietly saying, 'Yes, that is the current policy, and I think it is wrong, and I am not going to pretend otherwise,' and then taking whatever small action you can, questioning, escalating, voting differently, refusing to enforce it blindly.

It might mean writing the awkward email instead of muttering, 'That's above my pay grade.' It might mean leaving a job that pays very well because you realise your entire role is to make other people's lives slightly worse for no good reason. It might mean being the person who actually reads the contract and says, 'Hang on, why are we locking them into this penalty?'

It will not make you popular in beige rooms. It will, eventually, make those rooms slightly less toxic to human life.

FROM SPECTATORS TO PLUMBERS

If you want less cunthood, you need better plumbing. The good news, if we can call it that, is that you do not have to start by rewriting constitutions. You can start in the places you actually inhabit: your building, your street, your workplace, your club, your union, your school, your local party branch or tenants' group.

A building with decent plumbing does not rely on saints. It relies on routines. Agendas go out on time. Meetings occur at times when the majority can attend. Minutes are clear. Big decisions come with information attached. Roles rotate so the chair isn't a throne. Conflicts of interest are declared as boringly as you might declare a nut allergy. People can raise concerns without instantly being branded troublemakers or traitors.

It also relies on habits that look, from a distance, like weakness. Listening before you speak; letting the quiet person finish; asking the grumpy guy what he actually wants instead of guessing from his tone. Small peacemaking moves, repeated a lot, do more to keep a place liveable than any number of fiery speeches. None of that makes headlines. All of it makes it harder for the local petty tyrant or the 'helpful' manager to treat the whole joint as their personal fiefdom.

In politics, the same principle applies at scale. Systems that work accept that people are flawed, tempted, biased and sometimes thick as mince. They respond by building in checks, donation caps, independent watchdogs, public registers, real-time disclosures, courts that can say no when parliament loses its mind. That is not idealism. It is adult supervision. Decent plumbing also includes things like boring integrity measures, including transparent procurement, actual conflict-of-interest rules and watchdogs with teeth, not just logos. It means funding the ombudsman instead of defunding them because they were inconvenient this year. It means designing rules so that being merciful and fair is easier than being vengeful and sneaky.

If you are allergic to institutions, none of this will sound appealing. It shouldn't. Institutions are annoying. They are slow, weird, often pompous. They are also the only known way humans have found to offset the worst of our instincts with something like shared rules. The alternative is not 'freedom'. The alternative is every powerful bastard for themselves.

The plumber's mindset is not glamorous. It says, 'People are messy. I am messy. If we don't design this place with that in mind, the messiest people will run it.' It is humility dressed up as governance. It assumes that we will, at some point, be the ones making the mistake or losing our temper, and we'll be very glad the rails were there.

TURNING THE VOLUME DOWN, AND THE LIGHTS UP

Earlier we met affective polarisation, the shift from 'I disagree with those people' to 'I despise those people.' It is great for engagement metrics and terrible for everything else. It makes us easier to herd, easier to monetise and easier to distract. It also makes it much harder to hold anyone accountable, because we will forgive almost anything our own side does as long as they keep kicking the people we hate.

The cunts at the extremes live on attention. The cunts in the shadows live on inattention. Rebuilding the centre means learning, at whatever scale you can, to give the first group less attention and the second group less inattention. Locally, that might mean refusing to let every strata meeting turn into talkback radio. It might mean holding people to the agenda, politely cutting off monologues, insisting that complaints go via a process instead of via someone's Facebook crusade.

It might mean saying to the building's resident revolutionary, 'No, we are not turning this motion about window cleaning into a referendum on late-stage capitalism.'

It looks like phoning the angry resident before the meeting to hear them out, so they arrive slightly less nuclear. It looks like asking the quiet, reasonable person to speak early, so the room hears another tone before the first grenade gets lobbed. It looks like noticing when someone is being ganged up on and saying, 'Okay, one at a time,' even if you don't love them.

Civically, it might mean not sharing every bit of outrage-bait in your feed, even when it flatters your tribe. It might mean clicking on the boring article about actual legislation instead of the spicy take about how some minor council decision proves that civilisation is over. It might mean sending ten dollars and an hour of your time to a dull, competent local candidate instead of ten thousand retweets to a charismatic arsonist who makes you feel seen and achieves precisely nothing. It might mean muting the pundit whose entire career is live-tweeting their enemies' worst moments. It might mean not turning every difference of opinion into a character trial.

None of this is as satisfying as an online pile-on. That's the point. The thrill is part of the trap. Every time you let yourself be turned into a free content farm for someone else's rage machine, you are doing unpaid PR for cunthood.

Turning the lights up on the shadows is less dramatic and more repetitive. It is asking, whenever you can get away with it, who benefits and who decided, without immediately accusing anyone of satanic rituals. It is normalising, in your own circles, the idea that following the money and reading the paperwork is not paranoia but basic hygiene. It might mean showing up to the council budget meeting instead of just complaining later. It might mean reading the development application instead of sharing the meme. It might mean asking if anyone has checked the actual contract before the room rubber-stamps something that smells off.

If enough people treat those questions as ordinary, the shadows thin. Not because everyone becomes good, but because it becomes riskier and more annoying to be bad. Shadows thrive on two things: our laziness and our certainty that someone else is looking after it. The centre's job is to be just suspicious enough to read the fine print, and just kind enough not to turn that suspicion into permanent paranoia.

THE ADULT CENTRE, OR WHY THIS IS ALL SO BLOODY HARD

It would be nice to end with a rousing promise that if you do all this, temper your inner utopian, refuse to hide behind nouns, help fix the plumbing, starve the circus and light up the beige rooms, things will get steadily better. The truth is less cinematic. Things might get worse anyway. Climate collapse, pandemics, technological disruption, economic shocks, wars – none of these seemingly care how conscientiously you read your meeting papers.

What you get, if you're lucky, is not control. You get a fighting chance. You get a society where people still argue like hell, still disagree on fundamentals, still have wildly different lives, but where fewer decisions are made by unaccountable arseholes nobody elected. You get buildings where owners can disagree without suing each other, cities where planning laws mean something, economies where markets and states and civil society share power instead of taking turns playing god.

You get, in other words, an adult centre. Not a mushy middle that splits every difference, but a set of habits and institutions that make it possible to live together without worshipping purity or surrendering to shadows. Utopian cunts will tell you that's not enough. They will insist that anything short of total victory is betrayal. Shadow-cunts will hope you never even aim that high. They are quite happy with apathy and despair.

You are allowed to be disappointed by how modest the project sounds. 'Be slightly less of a cunt and help rebuild the centre' is not a slogan that will move units at a rally. It will not get you a statue. It will not make you feel heroic. It will mean losing arguments, backing boring people, reading documents and admitting that your enemies are still human beings with mortgages and bowel movements, dodgy knees, annoying relatives and the same late-night panic about bills that you have.

Someone far greater than me, offered the meek the chance to inherit the earth; what I'm pitching is a much smaller, grubby, local version of the same instinct. If enough of us choose, on purpose, to act a bit less like minor warlords and a bit more like decent neighbours, we probably won't save anyone's soul, but we might at least stop the worst people in the room from quietly buying the place out from under everyone else. No halos, no choirs, no stained glass windows – just the faint satisfaction of knowing you've made it fractionally harder for cunthood to run the table.

It will also mean copping flak. If you choose this path, you will, at some point, be yelled at for doing the right thing. You will be called a traitor by your own tribe for refusing to dehumanise the other one. You will be accused of weakness for practising mercy, and of arrogance for speaking up. Congratulations. That is more or less what it feels like to be a grown-up, and not a main character.

Nobody is coming to save you from them. But you do not have to become one of them to push back. You just have to be stubborn enough, humble enough and occasionally kind enough to keep showing up when it would be easier not to, and to keep acting as if other people are real even when they are behaving like NPCs in your personal tragedy.

That is how not to be a cunt, on purpose.

11

ARE YOU A CUNT?

There is, however, one person we've mostly let off the hook.

You.

Not the idealised you that nods along with all the good bits of this book. Not the future you who will definitely start going to meetings and reading documents, just as soon as you finish this paragraph and your life calms down. The actual you. The one who sends emails, sits in rooms, clicks buttons, ignores notifications, rolls eyes, votes, doesn't vote, shares, doesn't share and decides what is and isn't your problem.

So what follows is not a scientific instrument. It's a practical, slightly rigged exam designed to make you notice how you actually behave when nobody is writing a book about it. There are no marks, no certificates and no gold stars. There is only the question: When the bill for the common good arrives, do I quietly pay my share, or do I slide it to someone else? And a quieter question underneath: When it really stings, do I ever pay more than my share, on purpose?

You don't have to show your answers to anyone. You might not even want to admit some of them to yourself. That's fine. Start where you are.

Nobody becomes less of a cunt by pretending they have already arrived. They do it by finally admitting they're capable of better, and then paying for it in small instalments.

SECTION ONE: CONFESSION (MULTIPLE POOR CHOICES)

Imagine, for a moment, that your life had a CCTV system for decisions. Tiny cameras in your inbox, your browser, your meetings, your kitchen, your phone. I'm going to walk you through a few scenes. In each one, don't pick the answer you like. Pick the one you actually do.

In each scene, one option is entitlement ('my comfort first'), one is cowardice ('my skin first'), one is a costly move towards the centre ('I'll pay some of this bill'). Sometimes there's also a fourth thing humming underneath, a faint readiness to cop insult, awkwardness or boredom so someone else doesn't have to.

Scene One: The Meeting

You are in a meeting. It doesn't matter if it's a strata committee, staff meeting or parents' group. Someone opens their mouth and says something spectacularly stupid but mostly harmless. You feel your soul leaving your body.

What happens next?

A) You take a breath, let it pass, and steer back to the point because your goal is to get something done before you die. (Centre: you sacrifice the delicious hit of superiority so the room can stay workable.)

B) You correct them briefly, as kindly as you can manage, then move on. (Mixed: a small cost in awkwardness, but still mostly safe.)

C) You seize the opportunity to make a joke at their expense, win laughs from the people whose opinion you care about, and secretly enjoy that warm glow of superiority. (Entitlement: you sacrifice them for your moment.)

Scene Two: The Grubby Thing Your Side Did

Your preferred tribe – political, professional, cultural, whatever – has just done something obviously grubby but technically legal. Money from donors you shouldn't touch with tongs, something rammed through at 11 pm, complaints quietly shredded.

You read about it.

A) You immediately start defending them online, because the other side is worse and everyone should just shut up about it. (Cruelty: you sacrifice fairness so your team feels safe.)

B) You go quiet, feel a bit gross, and hope it blows over so you don't have to think about it. (Cowardice: you sacrifice conscience to keep your relationships tidy.)

C) You say, out loud, 'this is bullshit,' even if that means arguing with people who are supposed to be on your team. (Centre: you sacrifice tribal comfort to give the truth somewhere to stand.)

Scene Three: The Weak Person in the Way

In your building or workplace, a decision is on the table that will clearly hurt one weak person more than anyone else. The single mum who's behind on levies. The casually employed cleaner who will be 'let go' if costs need to come down. The person with a disability whose access ramp is about to be 'reconfigured' into a decorative planter.

You can see how this will land. So can everyone else.

A) You shrug. 'Rules are rules.' (Cowardice plus cruelty: you refuse even the smallest sacrifice of comfort to imagine an alternative.)

B) You feel bad but vote for it anyway. 'We can't make exceptions.

It's sad, but that's life.' (Cowardice: your reputation and convenience stay intact; they pay.)

C) You say, 'Hang on, is there any way we can do this that doesn't land so hard on them?', even though you know everyone will roll their eyes. (Centre: you sacrifice your popularity and the easy meeting to lessen someone else's hit.)

Scene Four: The Online Righteousness Binge

You see a post you violently disagree with. It is wrong on facts, wrong on tone, wrong on grammar and wrong on vibe. You can feel your thumbs tingling.

A) You keep scrolling because you are in a supermarket queue, and arguing with Greg from Geelong will not improve your life, his life or the power bill. (Centre: you sacrifice the high of rage so your attention can go somewhere useful.)

B) You type a fairly measured response, delete the most spiteful line, and hit send. (Mixed: small ego sacrifice, small contribution to sanity.)

C) You dive in hard – screenshot, subtweet, tags – and spend the next three hours refreshing for likes, seething that the other person 'just doesn't get it'. (Entitlement dressed as justice: you sacrifice time, strangers and any remaining nuance to feed your own heroic self-image.)

We could keep going.

Whether you quietly resent people on benefits without ever looking at a budget. Whether you share stories that are too perfect to check because they flatter your side. Whether you've ever thought 'they should not be allowed to vote' about an entire group, even in jest. Whether you talk a big game about justice and then treat the cleaner as scenery. Whether you ever make peace when you could make a scene.

You are not on trial. You are taking inventory. And your real politics, your real ethics, your real theology if you have one - that's not your slogan. It's what you actually bless with your behaviour.

SECTION TWO: DIAGNOSIS (WHERE YOU LIVE ON THE MAP)

Let's be generous and say you recognised yourself in at least one of those scenes. If you recognised yourself in none, put the book down and call a priest or a therapist because we have moved from cunthood to possible sainthood or delusion.

What Kind of Cunt Are You?

Some people bend towards the utopian extremes. You might not have a hammer and sickle tattoo or a 'Taxes Are Theft' bumper sticker, but you have a script. 'If only everyone did X, the world would be fine.' Your violence is mostly rhetorical, but the structure is the same: your sympathy shrinks around 'people like me', and everyone else becomes a problem to be solved. Entitlement is your main move. You won't sacrifice your certainty, your narrative, or your right to despise.

You will tell yourself you are hungry for justice. Sometimes you are. Sometimes you are just starving for confirmation that you are better than other people.

Other people bend towards the beige shadows. You would never dream of shouting at a protest, but you are surprisingly comfortable hiding behind the process. 'It's company policy.' 'We don't do it that way.' 'You have to understand, there are complexities.' You are unlikely to punch anyone. You are quite capable of signing something that ruins a life, then making a cup of tea and forgetting about it. Cowardice is your home base; you will sacrifice almost anything rather than your own smooth day.

You will tell yourself you are being realistic. Sometimes you are. Sometimes you are just hoping someone else will carry the cost of your realism.

Some of us, on bad days, are a cheerful blend of both. Revolutionary in tweets, bureaucratic in practice. We rage against the machine at night and oil its gears the next morning. We are, at the same time, outraged at how cruel everything is and weirdly resistant to any personal inconvenience that might make it slightly less cruel.

Again, none of this makes you uniquely monstrous. It makes you normal. That's why it matters.

Cunthood is not a separate personality type. It is what normal people become when their habits line up with the worst incentives available. The question is not 'am I a cunt?' The question is 'when the centre needs someone to pay a cost, do I reliably pretend the bill is addressed to someone else, or do I ever accept that being treated unfairly for doing the right thing is part of the deal?'

SECTION THREE: TRAINING (TINY, BORING REBELLIONS)

At this stage, you might be thinking, 'Fine, yes, I'm not perfect. What now?' This is the part where you expect a grand transformation, a new identity, a twelve-step program, a spiritual awakening.

No.

What you get instead is some tiny, boring rebellions. Because the problem we are dealing with is not a handful of cartoon villains. It is the sum of millions of tiny cowardices and unexamined entitlements. The only realistic counter is millions of tiny acts of sacrifice in the opposite direction. Think of it less as self-improvement and more as daily plumbing for your character.

Pick a few of these and actually do them. Not someday. This year. With witnesses.

Drill One: The Question You Don't Want to Ask

In your next heated argument online, in a meeting or at dinner, force yourself, once, to ask, 'What am I missing?'

You don't have to say it kindly. You don't have to agree with the answer. But you do have to ask it as if there might actually be something you don't know. This is not politeness. It is a small sacrifice of certainty. It costs you the pleasure of being completely right in your own head in exchange for keeping the door open between 'I disagree' and 'you are filth', and in that crack live most of the human possibilities other than war. It also trains a habit that doesn't get much airtime: being poor in your own wisdom and hungry for a reality check more than for another rhetorical win.

Drill Two: One Act of Visible Disloyalty

Within the next month, when your side, your party, your profession, your faction, your building clique does something obviously cooked, say so. Out loud. Where at least one other person can hear. You don't have to tweet a manifesto. You can start with 'that doesn't sit right with me', or 'if the other mob did this, we'd be furious'. The point is to break the reflex that says loyalty means never criticising your own.

This is a sacrifice of tribal safety. You risk side-eye, awkward chats, maybe fewer invitations. In exchange, you give the centre one more person who can say 'no' when the herd is charging. You also practise that deeply unpopular art: preferring what's right to what's comfortable, even when it feels like you're asking for trouble.

Drill Three: One Boring, Unrewarded Yes

Find some piece of dull civic plumbing and put your hand up. Stand for your strata committee or school council. Volunteer to read the by-laws and suggest actual edits. Join your union rep meeting instead of deleting the email. Go to the residents' forum. Turn up to the AGM when it isn't about a scandal.

You will be bored. You will meet tedious people. You will also sacrifice a night on the couch so the room is not left entirely to the most entitled, cowardly or cruel ones. Think of it as peacemaking with snacks, putting your body between the building and chaos, with nothing to show for it except the knowledge that things fell apart slightly less than they might have.

Drill Four: The Plaque Test

Before you sign, click or vote on anything that affects someone else's life, run a quick experiment in your head. 'If my name and face were printed next to this decision on a noticeboard, would I still be comfortable?'

If the answer is no, pause. Ask a question. Suggest an amendment. Buy time. Trigger a review. Refuse. Even one small action to reduce the harm is better than the shrug you normally give. This is a sacrifice of plausible deniability. You trade the comfort of 'I was just following orders' for the discomfort of owning your part. Over time, that habit is how ordinary people become quietly merciful, because they are allergic to doing invisible damage.

Drill Five: The Six-Month Question

When you are about to unleash your full righteous fury in an email, a meeting or a message thread, ask yourself, 'In six months, what would I rather have: the memory of this devastating takedown, or a slightly improved situation?' Sometimes the answer will be 'takedown'. You are human. Sometimes the answer, if you are honest, will be 'improvement'. Try to let that answer win often enough that your life starts to contain fewer glorious fights and more quiet wins.

This is a sacrifice of drama. You trade the story where you were magnificent for the reality where things are marginally less shit. You also give other people a way back from their worst moment, instead of nailing them to it forever.

SECTION FOUR: YOUR OWN ANTI-CUNT CONTRACT

At the end of a training session, you need something you can take away. But it is not a certificate; it's a contract with yourself.

You don't need to write a novel. You need three sentences you can put on a sticky note where your future self will see them: by your desk, on your fridge, above your toilet. Places where you make decisions, not where you perform being a good person. Something like the following:

- 'This year I will sacrifice at least one bit of tribal comfort by saying out loud when my side does something inherently wrong, even if it costs me.'
- 'This year I will sacrifice at least one evening to boring civic work instead of just complaining that nobody ever does the boring civic work.'
- 'This year I will not hide behind "that's just how it is" when I could ask one more question, even if that makes the room tense.'

If you're feeling ambitious, add one that hits your ego directly: 'This year, when I'm wrong, I will admit it without a ten-minute TED talk about my intentions.'

They don't have to be poetic. They have to be specific enough that, in twelve months, you can say whether you paid those costs or free-rode.

When the year is over, you do an audit. Where did you manage it? Where did you absolutely not? Where does your particular flavour of cunthood still refuse to sacrifice anything that actually hurts - your status, your serenity, your image? Then you start again. Not because you have failed, but because this was never a transformation montage. It is maintenance. You do not floss once and declare your teeth immortal.

The work is less like climbing a mountain and more like sweeping a floor. You do it. It gets messy. You do it again.

ANSWER SHEET: ARE YOU A CUNT?

SECTION ONE – CONFESSION: YOUR ACTUAL HABITS

Scene One: The Meeting

Tick the option that best describes what you actually do, most of the time:

- A
- B
- C

Then tick what you were chasing in that moment:

- My comfort (entitlement – getting the laugh, feeling superior)
- My safety (cowardice – avoiding awkwardness or conflict)
- The centre (paying a small cost so the room stays workable)

Reflection prompt (1–2 lines):

- When someone says something stupid-but-harmless, what's the *real* hit I don't want to give up (my joke, my image, my time, my calm)?

Scene Two: The Grubby Thing Your Side Did

Circle what you usually do:

- A
- B
- C

Tick what you were protecting:

- My team's image (cruelty dressed as loyalty)
- My social comfort (cowardice – avoiding difficult conversations)
- A shared standard (centre – truth gets a seat at the table)

Reflection prompt:

- When my side does something cooked, what do I sacrifice first: fairness, conscience, or tribal comfort?

____

____

____

____

Scene Three: The Weak Person in the Way

Tick what you usually do:

- A
- B
- C

Tick what you quietly decided about the weaker person:

- Their pain is acceptable collateral (cowardice + cruelty)
- Their pain is sad but "inevitable" (cowardice – I won't pay a cost)
- Their pain is a bill I'm willing to partially pay (centre)

Reflection prompt:

- Whose suffering am I most willing to ignore because they can't hit back?

Scene Four: The Online Righteousness Binge

Tick your most honest pattern:

- A
- B
- C

Tick what you were really buying:

- A hit of rage and superiority (entitlement dressed as justice)
- A small chance of usefulness (mixed motives)
- A bit of peace and freed-up attention (centre)

Reflection prompt:

- How many hours of my life have I willingly paid to feel "right" in front of strangers?

____

____

____

____

Extra Micro-Inventory (Tick All That Apply)

In the last 12 months:

- I've shared a too-perfect outrage story without checking it.
- I've thought an entire group "shouldn't be allowed to vote", even as a joke.
- I've talked a big game about justice, then treated service staff as scenery.
- I've quietly resented people on benefits without ever reading a budget.
- I've chosen making a scene over making peace when repair was possible.

For each box you tick, write one sentence:

- "The tiny cost I refused to pay here was _______________

____

____

____

_______________________________________."

SECTION TWO — DIAGNOSIS: WHERE YOU LIVE ON THE MAP

1. Your Default Bend

For each statement, rate yourself from 1 to 5, choosing the number that best fits you (1 = not me, 5 = painfully me).

Utopian / Entitled edge

- "If everyone just did X, the world would be fine."
  - 1 – Not Me
  - 2 – Rarely Me
  - 3 – Sometimes Me
  - 4 – Often Me
  - 5 – Painfully Me

- I need to feel morally smarter than "most people."
  - 1 – Not Me
  - 2 – Rarely Me
  - 3 – Sometimes Me
  - 4 – Often Me
  - 5 – Painfully Me

- I struggle to sacrifice my certainty or narrative, even for new facts.
  - 1 – Not Me
  - 2 – Rarely Me
  - 3 – Sometimes Me
  - 4 – Often Me
  - 5 – Painfully Me

Vanilla/ Cowardly edge

- "That's just how it is / policy / the process."
    ◦ 1 – Not Me
    ◦ 2 – Rarely Me
    ◦ 3 – Sometimes Me
    ◦ 4 – Often Me
    ◦ 5 – Painfully Me

- I value a smooth day more than a clear conscience.
    ◦ 1 – Not Me
    ◦ 2 – Rarely Me
    ◦ 3 – Sometimes Me
    ◦ 4 – Often Me
    ◦ 5 – Painfully Me

- I've signed or agreed to things I'd hate to see my name publicly attached to.
    ◦ 1 – Not Me
    ◦ 2 – Rarely Me
    ◦ 3 – Sometimes Me
    ◦ 4 – Often Me
    ◦ 5 – Painfully Me

Score each column (sum 3 items):
- Utopian / Entitled total: _____ / 15
- Vanilla / Cowardly total: _____ / 15

Quick read:
- Higher left score: You skew towards rhetorical violence and entitlement.
- Higher right score: You skew towards quiet, process-driven cowardice.
- Both high: Revolutionary at night, bureaucrat by day.
- Both low: Either doing surprisingly well or not being honest.

2. Your Cunthood Profile

Tick the phrase that feels closest:
- "I won't sacrifice being right."
- "I won't sacrifice being comfortable."
- "I won't sacrifice being admired."
- "I won't sacrifice being calm."

Then complete:
- "My particular flavour of cunthood is most obvious when ____

____

____

____

____

_______________________________________."

- "The bill I most reliably slide to someone else is ____________

____

____

____

____

(time, awkwardness, money, reputation, boredom, etc.)."

SECTION THREE — TRAINING: TINY, BORING REBELLIONS

Use this as a practical checklist for the year. The rule is simple: put a date when you actually do it, or leave it blank and face that honestly later.

Drill One — The Question You Don't Want to Ask

Target: Once in the next heated argument (online or offline), I will ask: "What am I missing?"

- Date I actually did this: ________________________________
- What I learned (one sentence): ____________________________

____

____

____

Drill Two — One Act of Visible Disloyalty

Target: Within a month, when my side does something obviously cooked, I will say so out loud to at least one person.

- Situation: ____

____

____

____

- Exact words I used (roughly): ____________________________

____

____

____

- Social cost I noticed (awkwardness, coldness, silence): ________

____

____

____

Drill Three – One Boring, Unrewarded Yes

Target: Commit one evening to dull civic plumbing (committee, AGM, union meeting, residents' forum, bylaws, etc.).

- What I turned up to: _______________________________________

  ____

- Date: _______________

- One small thing that was less shit because I was there: ________

  ____

Drill Four – The Plaque Test

Before a decision that affects someone else, ask: "If my name and face were printed next to this, would I still be comfortable?"

Use this mini-log three times:

1. Decision: _______________________________________

____

____

My answer to the plaque test: Yes / No
If "No", what I changed: _______________________________________

____

____

2. Decision: _______________________________________

____

____

My answer to the plaque test: Yes / No
If "No", what I changed: _______________________________________

____

____

3. Decision: _______________________________________

____

My answer to the plaque test: Yes / No

If "No", what I changed: ______________________________

____

____

Drill Five – The Six-Month Question

Before unleashing righteous fury, ask: "In six months, what would I rather have: the memory of this takedown, or a slightly improved situation?"

Two boxes to complete honestly:

- A time I chose takedown and would choose it again __________

  ____

- A time I chose improvement and was glad later: ____________

  ____

SECTION FOUR – YOUR ANTI-CUNT CONTRACT

Write three short, concrete sentences you can live with this year. Use these templates if helpful.

1. Tribal comfort

- "This year I will sacrifice at least one bit of tribal comfort by _____________________________________, even if it costs me

  ____."

2. Boring civic work

- "This year I will sacrifice at least one evening to boring civic work by _____________________, instead of just complaining about ____."

3. Process cowardice

- "This year I will **not** hide behind 'that's just how it is' when I could ____, even if it makes the room tense."

Optional ego clause:

4. Ego

"This year, when I'm wrong, I will admit it in one sentence, without a TED talk about my intentions."

End-of-year audit (for future you):

- Where did I actually pay a cost? _______________________

  ____

  ____

- Where did I absolutely refuse? _______________________

  ____

  ____

- My recurring pattern of cunthood looks like this: _________

  ____

  ____

Epilogue

THE TEN PRECEPTS OF NOT BEING A CUNT

When we started, the premise was blunt. You live in a world increasingly run, ruined and narrated by cunts. Some are loud, waving flags and manifestos. Some are quiet, shuffling papers in ordinary rooms. Most, on a bad day, look suspiciously like you.

We have wandered through utopian fantasists, racist fundamentalists, petty tyrants, corporate cowards, deep-state dreamers, strata warlords and shadow-cunts who thrive on our boredom. We have watched the centre thin out while everyone insists they alone are pure. We have tried, however reluctantly, to admit our own part in this carnival.

If this book has been anything, it has been a longwinded way of saying: 'Please, for the love of everything you claim to care about, try not to be a cunt.' You are tired. I am tired. So let's finish where we should have started – with the short version. Ten deliberately unholy precepts for how not to be a cunt, in public and in private, in buildings and in nations, and in your own head.

You will break them. I will break them. The point is not perfection. The point is direction.

Each precept is a fork in the road. One path is entitlement, cowardice or cruelty – a refusal to sacrifice anything that stings. The other is the centre – a willingness to pay some kind of cost so something shared can live, even if that leaves you looking small, hurt or unfashionably kind.

1. Thou shalt remember thou art not the main character.
You are the protagonist of exactly one story – your own. Everyone else is not the supporting cast, Non-Player Characters or background noise. They are running their own messy, frightened, hopeful lives at the same time as you.

Refusing this is entitlement; other people exist to orbit you. Accepting it is a sacrifice of grandiosity, and you give up your right to treat them as scenery so the world doesn't turn into your private stage. It is the basic humility of remembering that, in most rooms, you are the background to someone else.

2. Thou shalt not outsource thy conscience to a spreadsheet, a policy, or 'the market'.
When you are about to make or endorse a decision that obviously hurts actual human beings, you do not get to say that 'the system decided'. The system is wiring. You are the current.

Refusing responsibility is cowardice. You sacrifice strangers so your self-image stays clean. Owning it is a sacrifice of deniability, and you accept that your name is on the plaque so other people aren't just collateral. You don't have to fix every harm. You do have to stop pretending you had nothing to do with the one under your pen.

3. Thou shalt prefer boring fairness to exciting purity.
Pure solutions feel amazing. They are also how we keep driving off cliffs. Real life is full of trade-offs, half-measures and things that are better than before but less than perfect.

Choosing purity every time is entitlement; your feelings trump outcomes. Choosing boring fairness is a sacrifice of drama, and you give up the rush of total victory for the dull relief of things being slightly less shit for more people. You swap 'we won everything' for 'more kids eat, fewer people freeze', and you learn to live with the lack of a theme song.

4. Thou shalt argue hard without deleting someone's humanity.
Disagreement is inevitable. Contempt is optional. The moment your opponent becomes 'trash', 'vermin', 'Boomers', 'Karens', 'leeches', 'woke scum' or 'Nazis', you have given yourself permission to do almost anything to them in your head.

Dehumanising them is cruelty; you refuse to sacrifice even a sliver of empathy. Keeping their humanity in view costs you the pleasure of total contempt, but it keeps you anchored in a reality where repair is still possible. It means remembering that even the worst person you know still has a sick parent, a dodgy knee and a fear of dying alone.

5. Thou shalt ask 'who benefits?' and 'who decided?' without reaching for tinfoil.
Noticing patterns of power does not make you a conspiracy theorist. It makes you awake. Asking who writes the rules, who funds the campaigns, who keeps winning the contracts is basic civic hygiene.

Refusing to ask is cowardice; you sacrifice truth to stay comfortable. Asking costs you time, awkwardness and sometimes relationships with people who prefer the dark. You pay those costs so that cunthood in the shadows is slightly less safe. You treat transparency like smoke alarms: annoying until you need them, then suddenly essential.

6. Thou shalt do thy share of the boring work.
The centre did not die because nobody cared in the abstract. It died because not enough people could be arsed to sit in rooms, read papers

and vote for anything more demanding than a hashtag.

Free-riding on other people's effort is entitlement; you enjoy the public good without paying into it. Showing up is a sacrifice of leisure and attention so the worst people don't get the room to themselves. It is the unsexy peacemaking that stops every disagreement from turning into a court case or a coup.

7. Thou shalt keep thine own side honest.

If you only see corruption, stupidity and cruelty in people you already dislike, you are not principled. You are a fan.

Protecting your tribe at all costs is cruelty; you sacrifice justice so your team feels righteous. Calling bullshit on your own side costs you status and comfort inside the tent, and that cost is precisely what makes the centre real rather than a brand. You become the kind of person who would rather lose with integrity than win by quietly becoming what you hate.

8. Thou shalt match thy fury to the size of the offence, not the size of thy boredom.

Not everything is a five-alarm fire. Some things are just mildly annoying. Learning the difference is the basis of adult life.

Dropping nuclear reactions on parking-fine problems is entitlement. Your feelings demand the biggest stage available. Scaling your reactions to reality is a sacrifice of spectacle, and you give up some very good tantrums so that your anger still means something when it matters. You keep a little room in your emotional budget for the people who are genuinely being crushed, not just inconvenienced.

9. Thou shalt leave a path back from being a dickhead.

You will stuff up. So will everyone else. If your culture, workplace, building or friendship circle has no way for people to admit, repair and return, you are building a society of liars and hard cases.

Total, permanent banishment for every offence is cruelty disguised as justice. Leaving a path back costs you the satisfying story where you were right forever and they were wrong forever, but it gives the centre what it cannot survive without: the possibility of people actually changing. It means accepting that 'I'm sorry, I'll fix it' sometimes matters more than 'I'm right, and I always was'.

10. Thou shalt remember that 'less of a cunt' is a practice, not a personality type.
You will not wake up one morning and discover you have ascended to the Realm of the Non-Cunts. There is no badge, no moment of graduation, no point at which your work is done.

Treating decency as a fixed trait is entitlement; you refuse to sacrifice comfort by examining yourself. Treating it as practice costs you ego and excuses, and you accept that you will have to keep paying small, repeated prices – in time, attention, humility – for as long as you want to live as if other people are real.

It is, in the end, a life shaped by a simple, unglamorous belief. That the people who mourn what's broken, stay gentle under pressure, long for things to be fair, show mercy when they could crush, keep their motives clean, make peace in ugly rooms and cop shit for doing the right thing are not suckers, but the thin line between civilisation and a very loud, very stupid collapse.

You do not have to become a hero. You just have to become, stubbornly and on purpose, slightly less of a cunt than you were yesterday.

SELECTED BIBLIOGRAPHY

This book is not an academic work and nor does it purport to be, but the ideas in it did not appear out of thin air. They sit within a long tradition of historical writing, political thought, psychology and philosophy.

The works listed below fall into two categories. Some are the original sources for ideas that appear in these pages — the social contract, the psychology of obedience, the banality of institutional evil. Others are books that explore similar questions in greater depth, and which a curious reader might find worthwhile. None of them are required reading. All of them are worth your time if the arguments in this book sparked something you want to follow further.

Power and Political Reality

- Machiavelli, Niccolò. *The Prince.* Various editions; originally published 1532.
- Rousseau, Jean-Jacques. *The Social Contract.* Various editions; originally published 1762.
- Greene, Robert. *The 48 Laws of Power.* New York: Penguin Books, 1998.
- Schram, Stuart R., ed. *Mao Tse-tung: Talks and Interviews 1956–1971.* Harmondsworth: Penguin Books, 1974.

Authority and Human Behaviour

- Milgram, Stanley. *Obedience to Authority: An Experimental View.* New York: Harper & Row, 1974.
- Zimbardo, Philip G. *The Lucifer Effect: Understanding How Good People Turn Evil.* New York: Random House, 2007.
- Latané, Bibb, and John M. Darley. *The Unresponsive Bystander: Why Doesn't He Help?* New York: Appleton-Century-Crofts, 1970.
- Arendt, Hannah. *Eichmann in Jerusalem: A Report on the Banality of Evil.* New York: Viking Press, 1963.

Meaning, Responsibility and the Human Condition

- Frankl, Viktor E. *Man's Search for Meaning.* Boston: Beacon Press, 1946.
- Gibran, Khalil. *The Prophet.* New York: Alfred A. Knopf, 1923.
- Peterson, Jordan B. *12 Rules for Life: An Antidote to Chaos.* Toronto: Random House Canada, 2018.

History and Biography

- Beevor, Antony. *Stalingrad.* London: Penguin Books, 1998.
- Chang, Jung, and Jon Halliday. *Mao: The Unknown Story.* London: Jonathan Cape, 2005.
- Kershaw, Ian. *Hitler: A Biography.* New York: W.W. Norton & Company, 2008.
- Montefiore, Simon Sebag. *Stalin: The Court of the Red Tsar.* London: Weidenfeld & Nicolson, 2003.

ACKNOWLEDGMENTS

Every book begins long before the first word is written. It begins with the people you meet and the experiences that shape how you see the world.

So first, I would like to acknowledge all of the cunts I have encountered throughout my life. Across workplaces, institutions, politics, business, classrooms and the occasional dinner table, you provided more material than I could ever fit into one book. Your entitlement, cowardice and occasional flashes of cruelty were not always pleasant to experience at the time, but they were educational. This book would be much shorter without you.

To those who were certain I would never amount to much, thank you. Doubt can be surprisingly effective fuel.

I owe a special debt to the people who encouraged me to pursue my ideas even when they seemed unrealistic. My mother, Marie, whose faith in God and in me never wavered. She believed long before I did that I would one day write a book. My father, George, the most stubborn man I have ever met, who in many ways lived up to his name, the father of difficulty. To my dear friend Bernadette, who spent years urging me to keep writing and who edited everything I produced, except this. And my wife, Carla, whose patience and understanding made it possible to actually finish it.

Finally, I would like to acknowledge the Hembury Publishing team particularly. Jess Mudditt for eventually coming around to the idea and becoming supporters of the concept. When you decide to write a book titled *How Not to Be a Cunt*, the reception is not always immediately welcoming. Their willingness to look past the title and recognise the argument behind it helped bring this project to life.